FOCUS YOUR DAY

REFLECTIONS ON
CHRISTIAN EXPERIENCE

FOCUS YOUR DAY

Kenneth E. Grabner, C.S.C.

AVE MARIA PRESS   Notre Dame, Indiana 46556

FR. GRABNER deepened his contemplative perspective during his time as a Trappist monk. Now a member of the Congregation of Holy Cross, he currently serves on the staff of Fatima Retreat House at Notre Dame, Indiana, and as chaplain to the Holy Cross Brothers. His second book, *Awake to Life, Aware of God*, is also published by Ave Maria Press.

First printing, January, 1992
Third printing, January, 1998
30,000 copies in print

The bible text used in this publication is from the *Good News Bible*: Copyright © American Bible Society 1976. Used with permission. For the United Kingdom, permission granted by the British and Foreign Bible Society and Collins Publishers, London.

International Standard Book Number: 0-87793-467-3

Library of Congress Catalog Card Number: 91-76189

Cover and text design by Katherine Robinson Coleman

Printed and bound in the United States of America.

Preface

Christian life is both simple and complex. It is simple because its message is a single-pointed invitation to know and to experience the total love revealed in Jesus Christ. It is complex because we cannot embrace total love in one single experience. We can only taste it through a series of individual experiences. We can only understand it through a series of individual thoughts. If we reflect on our daily experiences and thoughts, they gradually form a whole in our lives and become a part of ourselves, defining who we are.

This book in an invitation to reflect on Christian experience day by day and to make the experience a conscious part of yourself. The reflections are short, for they are meant to be springboards for your own thoughts and meditations. Your personal meditation gives the Spirit of Jesus room to work within your life. Without that, Christian reading of any kind is not likely to bear much fruit.

Throughout this book, it has been necessary to use pronouns when referring to God, or to individual human persons. Unfortunately, the English language has no inclusive gender pronouns that can be used in the singular. The necessary use of gender pronouns in this book intends no masculine or feminine gender bias. My hope is that God will not be too confused by the gender assignments we give to him / her, and that those who read this book will find a value for themselves that transcends the limits of human language.

JANUARY

In God's Image

God created our world, and saw how good it was. That's what the book of Genesis tells us. But even if that book had never been written, we might have been able to guess its message by ourselves. If God did something, we would expect the results to be good.

When it comes to human beings, Genesis adds a further note to the goodness of God's creation. It says that human beings are made in God's image. That explains why you and I can act in this world with unselfish love, being a little like God and doing a little of what God does. God gives us this day and this new year as another possibility for growth, for love, for experiencing the peace that Jesus said only he could give. God entrusts us with time. The gift is not just for ourselves, but also for others. When this day ends and becomes a part of

7

our past, will we be able to say that we made something good of this day? If the opportunity were to be lost, how could it be recaptured?

Lord, may I truly live in your image, doing a little of what you do, and being a little of what you are.

JANUARY 2

Onyame

In Ghana, an often-heard word for God is the name, *Onyame*, pronounced awe-ny-a-may. The literal translation is, "He, who when you get him, you are fully satisfied." No other person, no other thing could ever logically receive such a name. That does not keep us from trying to apply that name to people and to things that are special to us. But the name betrays them, because they can never live up to its meaning. And if we misuse the name, we ourselves are betrayed.

If we know that *Onyame* is the name that belongs to God alone, we will simply let people be who they are, without placing demands on them that they are unable to meet. And we will let material things be simply what they are, instead of trying to make them into something they can never be. Those who know that *Onyame* is God's name alone will be the ones who can move through this world freely and unfettered. And no created thing will ever be able to deceive them.

Lord, you call me by name, and you allow me to call you by yours. Time will gradually reveal to

me something of what your name really means,
but may I come to understand more clearly each
day that only you can fully satisfy my life.

JANUARY 3

Climbing the Tree

Zacchaeus was probably the only contemporary of Jesus who was literally up a tree. His problem? Well, Zacchaeus was an extremely short man who had a burning desire to see Jesus. But in the midst of the large, curious crowd, he could see very little. And so, he got the idea to climb the tree.

His climb changed his life. He had made himself open and vulnerable, and so Jesus was able to touch him. "Hurry down, Zacchaeus, because I must stay in your house today" (Lk 19:5). Zacchaeus welcomed him with joy and said, "Listen, sir! I will give half my belongings to the poor, and if I have cheated anyone, I will pay him back four times as much" (Lk 19:8). There may have been a lot of people waiting to collect, but we can suppose that Zacchaeus' change of heart brought him joy. He became one with God and one with those among whom he lived. Perhaps his story is a paradigm of our own relationships with God.

Sometime in our lives, we will be called by God to do our own version of climbing the tree. The exact response to God's call will depend on our individual personalities and on the particular circumstances of our lives. The response will be different for each of us, but in the quiet openness of our hearts, we will recognize what it should be. And in responding, we will become capable of greater joy.

Lord, give me the courage to do my version of climbing the tree.

JANUARY 4

The Picture

When God created us, he had in mind everything we were meant to be, a kind of completed picture of what we could finally look like. The task of our life journey is to allow God to complete the picture. We do not know fully what it is, but for those who know the gospel, the basic outline is clear. We were created with the capacity to love, to be compassionate, and in a way, to be like God. To the extent that we become like that, people can look at us and see something of God. And we ourselves come to know the peace of Christ that lives within us.

But this may be asking for too much. How could we ever be like that? There is a lot of resistance in us. So when we finally allow God to work fully within us, the results may seem like a miracle. And yet this whole process is something that can begin to happen whenever we wish, even at this present moment, because God never stops offering us the power to be complete.

It's hard to believe, Lord, that this present moment is important enough to become a brushstroke in the overall picture of my life. Yet, nothing about me is unimportant to you. So, this moment is yours. I give it to you. Let it become a part of the final picture which is yet to be.

JANUARY 5

Useless Servants

"When you have done all you have been told to do, say, 'We are ordinary servants; we have only done our duty.'"

— Luke 17:10

This sounds like a divine put-down. After all of our labors and pains for God and for our fellow human beings, is this all that we can say about ourselves? Does God not realize the great cost to us as we begin to allow ourselves to be molded into loving persons and caring people?

But what if there were a more optimistic interpretation to these words of Jesus, so that they could be seen as a message of consolation and hope? Then they might mean that what Jesus asks of us is often not really all that difficult, and that we should not feel heroic or extraordinary in accomplishing his will. Conforming to God's loving plan for us would be an ordinary expectation, much in the same way as one ordinarily expects a seed to grow. The seed would do nothing heroic in sprouting and growing. It would simply unfold. And so we simply unfold, calmly becoming what we are meant to be. Nothing extraordinary. Just simply and joyfully doing what ought to be natural to us.

I give my life to you in trust, Lord. Whatever you ask of me, you give me the power to do. And so, if I accomplish something, I will be grateful for your help which makes all of my accomplishments possible. But I will not regard myself as special for having done what you so generously gave me the power to do.

JANUARY 6

Giving

When you were little, your parents probably never wondered, "What's the least I can do and still fulfill my obligations to this child?" Perhaps your childhood was filled not only with basic food, clothing, and education, but also with some extras and with an atmosphere of caring attention. You could have survived with less, but parental love gave you more. Even if you came from a dysfunctional family, and maybe we all did to some extent, you probably would have received more than just the bare necessities from someone in your life. To what extent do you share with others from the abundance of your own gifts?

There was a young man in the gospel who once asked Jesus how he could give of himself. Since the man had kept the commandments and done the basic things required in his life, Jesus decided to challenge him to a greater love. He invited the young man to sell everything he had and to follow him. The young man was not enthusiastic about the invitation, and he went away saddened. His refusal was tragic. It caused him to lose the joy that comes from giving more fully of one's life.

Is there a joy in life that comes from giving more than is strictly necessary?

Lord, you taught us that we would reap according to the measure in which we sow. Is my sowing adequate? Is there something more that others need from me that I have been unwilling to give?

J A N U A R Y 7

Gratitude

Jesus spoke up, "There were ten men who were healed; where are the other nine?"

— Luke 17:17

When Jesus cured the ten lepers, only one came back to give thanks. Had the other nine failed to realize the tremendous gift they had received? Even though they were cured, did they lose something by forgetting to be fully grateful?

More than the other nine, the leper who returned to give thanks would have had a clearer understanding of his relationship to Jesus. He would have been more aware of his healing as a personal gift. Would that have helped him to be more aware of the love of the healer?

We are continually surrounded by the gifts of God. We ourselves are gifts of God. Could gratitude add a profound dimension to the way we understand ourselves, other people, and the things of this world?

Lord, save me from the dullness of ingratitude.

The Price

When James and John asked Jesus if they could sit, one at his right hand, and the other at his left when he came into his glory, Jesus replied, "You don't know what you are asking for. Can you drink the cup of suffering that I must drink? Can you be baptized in the way I must be baptized?" (Mk 10:38).

"You don't know what you are asking for." Perhaps Jesus said that to James and John because they weren't sufficiently aware of the price that would have to be paid for a request such as theirs. And from that point of view they did not know what they were asking. Did they perhaps want the glory without fully accepting the suffering, the reward without fully accepting the struggle? Maybe they were like those who want to become star athletes, but without the training. It never seems to work out.

There is a path that leads to glory with Jesus. It is a path of service, a giving of the self, a letting go of the ego. It is a path of compassion, a willingness to listen to others and to ease their pain at the expense of our own time and energy. The experience of the peace that only God can give comes when we do those things. That seems to be how we get ready for the glory.

*Lord, I'm not very courageous. I'm not sure I
can be fully baptized into your baptism, but I
will live my life as well as I can, one day at
a time. Help me to die to myself that I might
live unto you.*

JANUARY 9

Identity

Many people seem to need honors and recognition
in order to feel alive. They find their identity in
those things. Jesus tells us often in the gospel that
our real identity can only be found in the things
we sometimes don't think about or care to do. We
find our true identity as Christians when we serve
the needs of others, and when we do that with a
sense of genuine love. And we find our identity
in an even deeper sense from the understanding
that we are God's children, that God's life is our
life. When we finally grasp that, we no longer need
honors, positions, and success as the world sees it.
We become free from those things.

The big question, though, is whether we really
want to be free. Do we really want to be without our
illusions? How does a hypochondriac ever give up
his medicine when he is convinced that he needs
it to live? And how does a person ever give up
illusory values if she is convinced she needs them
to survive?

*Lord, make my illusions known to me. Even
when I finally discover them, I know that I
cannot be free of them without the strength of*

your help. Grant me true freedom, your gift to
all of your children who sincerely seek it.

JANUARY 10

Blindness

People who can't see are often in danger of bumping into things. Unfortunately, reality never rearranges itself for the convenience of the blind. That may be a cruel fact of life, but not much can be done to change it. The same is true for the psychologically and spiritually blind.

Where does our blindness hurt us and get us into trouble? Spiritual blindness reveals its harmfulness through its symptoms. Sometimes the symptoms show themselves as unreasonable sadness, anger, or anxiety, or at other times perhaps through a vague and persistent dissatisfaction with life.

Many people are reluctant to take the time to understand the possible meaning of those symptoms when they discover them. But if they do, they become wise. The gospel always challenges people on their reluctance to be wise.

Lord, do I sometimes cause my own suffering by my refusal to see and accept life as it is? Give me your Spirit, the Spirit of wisdom, that I might see something of what you see. I hold my blindness up to you. Give me sight.

Who Are You, Jesus?

Is Jesus primarily the Son of God who judges us? Is he someone who died for us once, but who no longer has much power in our lives, someone who perhaps no longer has a compelling meaning for us?

Or is Jesus the Son of God who genuinely loves us? Someone who is truly our friend and who comes into our lives with moving power and presence?

In reality, Jesus can only be who he says he is. We can either accept him that way, or else we can create an illusion, a caricature of who he says he is.

Jesus once asked his disciples who they thought he was. Peter answered, "You are the Messiah, the Son of the living God" (Mt 16:16). That understanding remained all through Peter's life, but cannot we suppose that the understanding grew in depth? As Peter's daily experience of Jesus grew, so did his understanding of who Jesus really was.

Perhaps no one can give his or her complete and final answer to the question of who Jesus is. The answer is open-ended. Its richness grows according to the depth of one's faith and the daily experience of Jesus' love.

Lord, free me from my illusions. Send your Spirit upon me. Lead me to understand your word and your presence in my life, that I might see you as you are and grow in the peace that only you can give.

Prayer

A Pharisee and a tax collector each offered a prayer. The Pharisee thanked God that he was not like the tax collector. The tax collector's prayer was quite different. He just humbly asked for God's mercy. It was the tax collector's prayer that received the approval of Jesus.

Both the Pharisee and the tax collector revealed themselves by the way they prayed. In a similar vein, your way of praying reveals something about yourself. It also reveals the way you look at God. And, of course, if you do not pray much, that reveals something too.

If your prayer is just a rote activity, do you really look at God as your friend? If you rarely thank him, do you see him as the source of all you have? If you only pray when you need something, do you really love your God? If you rarely think about God during your day, is God really at the core of your life? Examine the way you pray. A clearer idea of who you are will begin to emerge.

Lord, I want to know your presence in every phase of my life, and I acknowledge that this desire is your gift. You want me to know your presence far more than I desire to know it. Teach me to be aware of you, and that will be prayer. Help me to be quiet with you, even for a few minutes, and that will be prayer. Allow me to serve others in your name, and that too will be prayer. Thank you, Lord.

Perceptions

Jesus liked to turn things upside down. When he told the story about the Pharisee and the tax collector, he put the best prayer in the tax collector's mouth. Would it not have made more sense to put the best prayer in the mouth of the Pharisee? Pharisees were educated in Jewish law and respected by the people. They would have been expected to offer a good prayer. But who would have had similar expectations from a tax collector?

Perhaps Jesus' story is a paradigm of life, a kind of humorous lesson that people and things are not always what they seem to be. God can be found in the unlikeliest people and in the strangest places. His love works in people that sometimes we may not care much about. Perhaps Jesus wants to challenge us about the way we look at others, to see beauty in people whom we never would have expected to be beautiful at all.

Where my perceptions of others need to be changed, Lord, I ask you to help me change them. Let me see others through your eyes.

Appreciation

An elderly woman lived alone in a dingy, old hut. She complained loudly about its lack of amenities, and her fairy godmother was moved with pity. With a swish of her wand, she changed the hut into a comfortable cottage. But the elderly woman complained that the cottage was too small, and so her fairy godmother changed the cottage into a large house. Now the woman complained that with such a large house, she could not possibly live comfortably without several servants. So the fairy godmother went all out for the woman, and with a grand swish of her wand, changed the house into a huge palace complete with servants. But this time, the elderly woman complained that the servants were lazy, and that too much of the palace management fell on her alone. Exasperated, the fairy godmother cut through the air with a final swish of her wand, and the elderly woman found herself back in the dingy, old hut.

Rich or poor, this woman seemed determined to be unhappy. Some might say that if you are going to be unhappy anyway, you might as well be unhappy while being rich. But, finally, it did not really matter. Because of the woman's inability to appreciate anything, everything was lost to her. What good are the gifts of life if their goodness is not appreciated and enjoyed?

Lord, help me to be more aware of your goodness that so often comes to me through people and through the things in life you allow me to enjoy. Deepen my appreciation for your gifts.

JANUARY 15

Motivation

Three young men decided to enter medical school, each one for quite different reasons. One entered because he thought he would enjoy the work. The second man entered because he thought that this profession would give him a very good life. The third entered because he genuinely cared for people and wanted to spend his life alleviating suffering. Three different men; three different motivations.

For most people, the question of motivation may not be as clear-cut as it was for the three young medical students. Perhaps most people's motivations for doing things are mixed. The work they do is for their own good, but it is also for the good of others. But which motive predominates? The gospel challenges all of us to see if our primary motivation is love.

In what we do, do we really love God with all our heart, soul, mind, and strength? Do we love our neighbors as ourselves?

Lord, a lot of what I do is mostly for my own benefit, and many times I'm not even aware of that. May I learn more deeply to make my work an offering to you and a service to others.

J A N U A R Y 16

Choices

An old Russian tale says that the inhabitants of heaven and hell both sit at tables loaded with delicious food. The ground rules for the feast are that the diners must eat with extremely long-handled forks, and that they must grasp the forks at the end of the handle. The people in hell starve because they cannot figure out how to feed themselves that way. But, for the people in heaven, this is not a problem.

They simply reach across the table and feed each other.

The inhabitants of heaven and hell live with the attitudes they had while they were on earth. The story is a reminder of the importance of what we do in the present moment. Our choices make us who we are, not only for this life, but also for the next. Our everyday thoughts and actions can have tremendous consequences, reverberating into eternity.

Help me to remember, Lord, the full meaning of what I do today.

JANUARY 17

Suffering

Although we prefer to have God speak to us through our joys, we often hear his voice through our sufferings. Our sufferings often tell us that all is not right with our lives. If we are unable to forgive, our bodies can signal their protest through pain, a sign that something needs to be changed. A great number of spiritual problems make themselves known through the breakdown of the body and the unraveling of the emotions. God speaks to us through that pain, using it to call us to a healthier way of being.

People are not responsible for all of their suffering, of course, but they might be responsible for a good deal of it. Once people learn how they cause some of their suffering by unhealthy mental attitudes, they can be healed. Freedom comes when people learn to understand that sometimes they are their own worst enemies.

Enlighten me, Lord, that I might understand what you say to me through my sufferings. Help me to learn and to be healed.

JANUARY 18

Predicaments

When the wine supply was exhausted at the wedding feast at Cana, Mary simply said to Jesus, "They are out of wine" (Jn 2:3). There was nothing Mary could do about it, but she knew that there was something Jesus could do. And so she addressed the servers, saying, "Do whatever he tells you" (Jn 2:5). From Mary's humble request came the miracle freeing the bride and groom from the embarrassment of having no wine.

How many times in life do we share Mary's predicament? Something needs to be done, but we are unable to do it. We can either respond angrily or passively to our own impotence, or we can humbly ask for God's help. Some situations in life can best be handled by putting them in the hands of God. And if there is something more that God wants from us, our attentiveness to his inspiration will make it clear to us what we are to do.

Into your hands, Lord, I place all the predicaments of my life. I will handle the ones that I can, and I trust you to handle the ones that I cannot.

Ordinary Things

It seems to be a principle of life that God usually comes to us in very ordinary ways. Dandelions are far more prevalent than roses. Sparrows are more common than canaries. People with personality flaws are far more common than those who do not have them — if indeed there is anyone who does not. Jesus himself seemed quite ordinary to his relatives, and so they missed his significance. God does come and speak to us in the ordinary everyday persons and events in our lives. If we wait for someone or something else, then we will miss God.

Lord, teach me not to write off the seemingly ordinary persons and events of my life, for that is all I have, and where else are you to be found? When I discover more deeply that you are in everyone and in everything, the ordinary will cease being simply ordinary. Then I will see all persons and things for what they are — bearers of your presence.

Personal Experience

The Bible is a written record of certain people's experiences of God. God revealed himself to them and later the experiences of the revelation were put into words. We are left with the words. The challenge is to turn the words back into a personal experience, analogous to the original experience that was written and recorded for us. All of Jesus' stories and teachings, all of Paul's writings, in fact, the entire written word of God is meant to lead to our own personal experience of God. How does this happen?

Put yourself into the biblical stories and experience them as happening to you. For example, you might read the story of the storm on the lake (Mt 8:23–27). Imagine yourself in the boat with Jesus and the disciples as the waves threaten to engulf you. You wake Jesus up and watch him calm the storm. How might this apply to your own life, and what would you say to Jesus about that? What would Jesus say to you? How would you apply Jesus' teachings to your life and allow them to become living experiences?

Lord, I want to take the time to discover the living reality embedded in your word, that I might come to a personal experience of what you have revealed.

JANUARY 21

Caring

"John the Baptist sent us to ask if you are the one he said was going to come, or should we expect someone else?" At that very time Jesus healed many people from their sicknesses, diseases, and evil spirits, and gave sight to many blind people. He answered John's messengers, "Go back and tell John what you have seen and heard: the blind

25

can see, the lame can walk, those who suffer
from dreaded skin diseases are made clean,
the deaf can hear, the dead are raised to
life, and the Good News is preached to the
poor."

— Luke 7:20–22

Jesus said that people could understand his powerful care for them by what he did. The blind
were seeing, the lame were walking, and the poor
were hearing the Good News. Do these things still
happen, or were these powerful events restricted
mainly to Jesus' time?

In our day, it does seem that the wonders
of healing still occur through prayer, but many of
these wonders also happen through our own caring
actions toward others. Jesus gives us the strength to
care about the poor, those who are anxious or sad,
those who feel unwanted. Through the power of
Jesus working within us, people begin to be healed.
The caring of Jesus is still powerful and present
whenever we respond to his love by showing compassion to our neighbor.

*Today, Lord, I would like to be a channel of
your healing power. Help me to respond to
those who are in need of your peace.*

JANUARY 22

The Kingdom

Jesus said that the kingdom of God is within us. The
kingdom is not something we create or construct

out of brick or stone. It is rather the loving presence of God, and our happiness consists in becoming aware that this presence is always with us. When we live the love that flows from God's presence within us, we radiate the kingdom to others. The kingdom becomes more visible each time the love inside of us incarnates itself through caring actions.

Jesus, I want to make visible for others the king-dom you have placed within me. Help me to incarnate your love in the midst of the people with whom I live and work.

J A N U A R Y 23

Acceptance

We can never command God to come into our lives, but we can create an inner space that makes it possible for us to notice who is already there. How can that be done? Perhaps the most meaningful way is to accept the present moment with love, and, after doing our best, to avoid craving for things to be other than they are. We would still work for what is good and just, but there would be a calm acceptance of the results, no matter how meager or disappointing. Such an attitude would leave us free, open, and uncluttered. The mind would be still, and in the calmness, there would be a greater awareness of the presence of God, with the strength for new beginnings.

Lord, teach me to accept the results of what I do, that I might be free and unencumbered. I want to prepare for you in calmness. May

I not drown out the awareness of your presence through my dissatisfactions and noisy cravings.

JANUARY 24

Patience

When Jesus cured the blind man of Bethsaida (Mk 8:22–26), the cure did not come all at once. After Jesus touched the blind man's eyes, he asked, "Can you see anything?" The man replied, "I can see people, but they look like trees walking around." It was necessary for Jesus to touch the man's eyes a second time before he could see perfectly.

Perhaps the blind man's experience is a paradigm of our own. Growth toward wholeness and understanding is usually a gradual process, although we might wish it were otherwise. We have to die to something unwholesome within ourselves before our healing is complete. Even when we discover our own self-imposed obstacles, the process may be slow. Can we be gentle and patient with ourselves? And also with others who share the same struggle to become whole?

I may be too impatient with myself and with others, but, Jesus, you are very patient with me. Help me to learn from you, you who called yourself "meek and humble of heart."

In Accord With God

Peter and several of the apostles had spent the entire night fishing, but when morning came, their net was empty. Jesus stood on the shore and called out to them, "Throw your net out on the right side of the boat, and you will catch some." So they cast their net, and they caught so many fish that they could not haul the net in (Jn 21:1–6).

This is a story about the power of God in the midst of the frustrations of life. One never knows exactly when or in what way this power comes.

A little girl was in a serious automobile accident that necessitated the amputation of her leg. After the operation, she called in a nurse and asked her to pray that God would restore the leg. The nurse held the little girl, and prayed that God would be with her, and that he would help her to live her life as best she could, no matter how it turned out.

Perhaps the "catch of fish" in the girl's case would have been the power from God to accept her life as it was, and to make of it absolutely everything that she could. That would have been a miracle equal to the catch of fish any day. People who love and radiate joy to others in the midst of their own unfortunate circumstances are always miracles. Their love and acceptance of their lives is a great gift to those of us who can learn from their courage.

I ask for the miracle, Lord, to peacefully accept those things that I cannot change.

Quiet

The Bible tells us that Jesus prayed often, and that at times, he would withdraw to be alone with his Father. The human nature of Jesus felt this need for quiet communing with God, and Jesus took time for it, despite the pressing needs of so many people around him.

The temptation is to think that our service to others is compromised if we give much more than token time to quiet prayer. Perhaps the opposite is true. Prayer puts us in touch with the presence of Jesus within us. Awareness of his presence is the light that teaches us how to serve others according to his mind, and it is the strength that enables us to serve them with his love. In this sense, time taken for quiet prayer is an essential part of our caring for others.

My priorities are easily confused, Lord. Although I try to find you in the noisy parts of my life, I often forget to find you in the quiet ones. Help me to achieve a sense of balance, so that I might discover you more deeply, and serve you more completely.

Trust

"Oh no, sir," answered the officer. "I do not deserve to have you come into my house.

Just give the order, and my servant will get well."

The speaker was a Roman centurion, and he asked Jesus for a cure. He did not ask for the reassuring gesture that would have come from Jesus' physical contact with his son. The method of healing was left up to Jesus. The trust was complete. Jesus marveled at the centurion's faith.

Perhaps our own faith is somewhat different. We ask for God's help and then we tell him exactly how he should go about giving it. We have preconceived ideas as to how God should respond to us. Even with God, we try to remain in control. But did you ever notice that the more you try to control your life, the more out of control it gets?

Lord, I entrust my life and my concerns for others into your hands. I trust you to answer my prayers in the way that is best.

J A N U A R Y 28

Open To Receive

"Sir, don't trouble yourself. I do not deserve to have you come into my house, neither do I consider myself worthy to come to you in person. Just give the order, and my servant will get well."

— Luke 7:6–7

31

The centurion's words carry a further message from the one looked at yesterday. The centurion knows he is not worthy, but he still hopes to receive something. He trusts in Jesus' love, rather than in his own worthiness.

God does not respond to us because we are worthy. He responds to us because he loves us. If you are willing to receive God's love, then you already have it. And when you have it, you are worthy, because God's love makes you that way.

Let us put away the idea that we can ever earn God's love. Who can earn what has already been freely given? It is simply there. Our response is just to accept what is already present, and to be grateful for what has been freely given.

Nothing to earn; everything to accept. It seems a strange way for things to be, Lord, but your thoughts are quite different from ours. I won't try to figure them out. I will just accept you as you say you are.

JANUARY 29

Resentments

Resentments are some of the greatest killers of joy. They constrict our vision and turn us back on our own hurts. Ultimately, they rob us of the possibilities of growth and leave us with only a shell of what we could be.

Resentments come wrapped in different colors and varieties. Individuals who hurt us, institutions, even life itself — all of these can provide the stuff for attitudes of well-nurtured hostility. In the end, the particular variety of the resentment may not matter that much. The spiritual and psychological results are deadly no matter what variety it takes.

The Christian message invites us to let go of resentments so that we might lessen our pain and experience a renewal of life. Letting go of our resentments may be a painful process, but it would be even more painful to hang on to them.

I know that my resentments cause a hemor-rhaging of my vitality, and that they hurt only myself. And so I ask for the power to give them up, that I might become free and whole.

J A N U A R Y 30

Mind Power

A large part of our day is already programmed before the day even starts. We do the programming, and our minds set us up for the way we react to what happens along the course of our day. Both positive and negative mindsets produce their own unique kinds of tone that influence our daily experience.

The power of our minds to determine the tone of our day is tremendous, and so it makes sense to realize what our minds are doing. If we pay attention, we may catch ourselves thinking negative thoughts. Once we are more fully aware of doing that, we can change the habit. The way our day turns out is, in part, up to us.

*I ask the grace of greater awareness, Lord, that
I might be more conscious of my thoughts and
of the direction in which they lead me.*

JANUARY 31

The Future

A chick just starting to peck its way out of its shell
can only be aware of what is inside the shell. Human
beings live in a kind of shell too, a shell of
space and time, and their consciousness of what
lies outside is dim. But at death, the shell cracks
and they are liberated from its confines into a fuller
kind of consciousness. They experience the resurrection.

We try to live fully in the present moment, doing
our part to form a community of peace and
justice that radiates the love and presence of God.
But at the same time, we believe in all the promises
of the gospel, hoping for the full freedom of the
future, when we shall be liberated from the shell
of space and time. We look forward to the full life
that will be ours through the promise of the resurrection,
for this promise adds meaning and joy to
our present moment.

*Teach me not to doubt or dismiss your promises
about eternal life, Lord, but rather to trust enthusiastically
in your magnificent generosity.*

FEBRUARY

FEBRUARY 1

One of a Kind?

People suffer greatly whenever they imagine that their embarrassing fantasies and idiosyncrasies are unique. Priests, ministers, rabbis, and counselors who do a lot of listening know that no personal problem is ever unique.

Legions of people struggle with the same problems as you do. Of course, they usually hide that fact, and so you may tend to think that your thoughts and your problems are common only to you. But, considering the billions of people walking with you on the path of life, how could anything you think or do be totally unique?

You know I'm not alone in my problems, Lord, no matter how embarrassing or horrendous they seem. Many people carry burdens similar to mine, and we are all united in the reality of your compassionate love.

FEBRUARY 2

As You Will It, Lord

Jesus taught us to pray for our daily bread and for all our other needs as well. Is this teaching sometimes misunderstood? When Jesus prayed in the garden of Gethsemane that his cup of suffering might pass, he added the words, "Yet not what I want, but what you want" (Mt 26:39).

Some people pray that God will do their will. Others pray that they might do the will of God. It is from the latter kind of prayer that life's greatest miracles occur.

"Your will be done on earth as it is in heaven."
May I mean it, Lord, and come to know your
peace through my trust in your love and wisdom.

FEBRUARY 3

Criticism

Critics can be more valuable than friends, because critics say openly what friends sometimes hide. Critics put us in touch with parts of ourselves that we might never discover on our own.

Paradoxical as it may seem, constructive criticism can open the way for greater contentment, because it makes us aware of what needs to be changed in ourselves. If the change makes us happier persons, the criticism will have been a gift to us.

I tend to close up when I'm criticized, Lord. Help me not to turn away from people who constructively challenge me, but rather to hear what needs to be heard.

FEBRUARY 4

Where Are You, God?

If the presence of God can be seen through creation, why is God so often missed? Is there a problem, perhaps, with the way we see?

How many of us are able to look at spring flowers or autumn foliage without thinking of something else while we look? But if we are thinking of something else, how can we detect the presence of God while looking at what God has made?

What we sense of God today will depend on how attentive we are when we look. If our minds are somewhere else, we will not have fully seen what is in front of us.

My mind is rarely still, Lord, and so it misses you. Today I will look with a calm mind, so that my seeing may reveal something new.

FEBRUARY 5

Recollection

If we love Jesus, we sense a growing desire within ourselves to know the life-giving experience contained in his words. The life-giving experience comes, in part, through our service to others, in imitation of Jesus. But what kind of service can there be without a recollected and loving heart?

Spend quiet time with your God, and your God will teach you the kind of love that will open your heart. And when your heart is opened, true service to others will follow as a natural consequence. All things of value find their genesis in the silence of a heart open to receive the inspiration of the Spirit of Jesus.

Would the effectiveness of my service be greater, Lord, if I learned to be quiet with you for a period of time each day? May I come to understand more clearly the value of my silent moments with you.

FEBRUARY 6

Forgiveness

Some of Jesus' contemporaries were amazed at his spirit of forgiveness. Had we heard his words and seen his actions, would we have been amazed too? Forgiveness comes hard to us. And whenever we tend to think that God is like we are, we think that his forgiveness is too good to be true.

Jesus forgave prostitutes and thieves. He even forgave Peter who denied him, and those who put him on the cross. Would there be any reason to doubt that his compassionate love touches us too? And if this is true, what does this say about the need for us to be compassionate and forgiving toward others?

*The only ones who don't receive your forgive-
ness, Lord, are those who don't want it. I
believe that you are a forgiving God because
that's who you say you are. Deepen my faith
in your compassionate forgiveness, and help me
to imitate you in forgiving others.*

FEBRUARY 7

Expectations

When Jesus forgave sinners, he said to them, "Go
and sin no more." He had an expectation of them.
The expectation was born of love. Where there is
no love, there is no expectation.

Jesus understands the scars and the personal
conflicts that can result in selfishness. But he still
hopes for and expects a change, while continuing
to love even when no change comes. This is the
way our compassionate God loves, with a love that
invites us to wholeness. It is the way God asks us
to love those who need our forgiveness.

*Your expectations of me are not meant to be
burdens, Lord, but rather invitations to become
whole. May I see your expectations for what
they are, acts of compassionate love.*

FEBRUARY 8

Doing Your Best

A group of athletes preparing for a race ordinarily would not arouse much curiosity. But one fact

marked this particular group of athletes as different — they were all in wheelchairs. Perhaps at one point in their lives, being without legs would have been cause for self-centered anger and bitterness. These athletes decided to die to those attitudes that they might become alive to more satisfying ones. Their creative use of their sufferings and limitations inspired all those who witnessed their determination.

Most of us are burdened with some kind of physical, emotional, or spiritual limitation. How do we react? If we decide to live as fully as we can in spite of our sufferings and limitations, then we already know a foretaste of the resurrection, a new way of living that broadens our horizons and brings us joy.

Lord, may I rediscover the joy of making the best of what I have.

FEBRUARY 9

Enduring

Jesus explained his cross, the giving up of his life, as an act of love for his friends. His friends could no longer consider the mystery of the cross and still wonder if Jesus really loved them. The endurance of Jesus spoke powerfully about the quality of his love.

Would that also be true for us? What would be the quality of our love if we were never willing to endure anything for it? In fact, there probably is no genuine love without suffering. How many times have you discovered this in your own relationships with your family and community?

You give an example of love, Jesus, which is hard to follow. Help me to bear love's burdens so that my caring may be genuine and life-giving.

FEBRUARY 10

Life Through Death

"If anyone wants to come with me, he must forget himself, take up his cross every day, and follow me. For whoever wants to save his own life will lose it, but whoever loses his life for my sake will save it."

— Luke 9:23–24

What a paradox! How could one begin to make sense out of it? And yet, is there something in this that is validated by our own experience?

Perhaps you noticed a greater joy in your life whenever you genuinely cared for others at some cost to yourself. In those moments, you knew a satisfaction that self-centered people never experience. You felt fulfilled. You were more fully alive.

Jesus invites all of us to the fuller life that comes from a deeper experience of loving. That gift is ours when we decide to accept Jesus' invitation to live as he did. In the acceptance of his invitation, we grow toward the fullness of who we are meant to be.

Dying to myself comes hard for me, Jesus. But, according to your word, it is in dying to ourselves that we are born into a deeper experience of life. If there were any other way, certainly you would have shown it.

FEBRUARY 11

Accepting Yourself

Can you remember your school days? It might have seemed that some of your classmates were lucky. They learned quickly and retained what they learned. Then there were others who got hardly anything at all and remembered even less. Most fell somewhere in the middle. If each one did his or her best, that should have been enough. But at times, more was expected of some than they were able to give.

Jesus calls us all to be his disciples, but some are better learners than others. At any given moment, we follow as best we can, and God accepts what we are able to give. If we believe this, we won't berate ourselves for not having spiritually arrived. God simply asks for our best, a "best" that may not yet be perfect.

Perhaps the "A" students are a minority among Jesus' followers, but there are many people struggling to love as much as they can. They should be content. God is.

Teach me, Lord, to accept myself as you accept me.

Following Jesus

We call ourselves Christians because we follow Jesus. Jesus spent his time among us offering hope and love, alleviating suffering, and finally giving his life for the sake of our own. The actions of Jesus make it clear what we ourselves should do, for his life is meant to be a paradigm of ours.

What would it mean in your particular circumstances to offer hope and love to others, to alleviate their sufferings, to offer your life for the sake of others? Which people need to receive the caring that you alone can give? What concrete things would you do for them? Is there something that others need from you that you are not giving to them?

Lord, may I not rest in a dreamy kind of discipleship that is full of good thoughts, but which never accomplishes much for anybody. Through my receptivity to your inspiration, may I be of genuine service to others.

Compassion

God understands the sinner because God understands the reasons, the struggles, and the circumstances that accompany sin. That never means that the sin is condoned. It simply means that God is compassionate toward the sinner.

We are unable to understand all of the reasons, the struggles, and the circumstances that accompany sin. That is true as much for the sins of others as it is for our own. And so God tells us not to judge others, because we never have all the facts. God, who does have all the facts, is a forgiving and compassionate God. We are made in God's image. To be lacking in forgiveness and compassion is to forget in whose image we are made.

I will not forget in whose image I have been made, Lord. Help me to break the unyielding crust around my heart that keeps me from being compassionate and forgiving.

FEBRUARY 14

A Matter of the Heart

This is the day when people send the cards with the little hearts on them. Love is so important in human life that society feels a need to set aside a special kind of day to celebrate it. It is a good time to recommit ourselves to those we love, and a good time to remember someone who otherwise might not receive any sign of love at all.

People can only celebrate this day according to the way they understand the meaning of love. If love means a committed, unconditional caring that goes beyond feelings, then this day commemorates what is best in human relationships. People who share that kind of love have an incomparable treasure. They reveal to one another an image of the love of God.

44

Thank you, Lord, for all of the love I've received, and for all of the love I've been able to give. Thank you for your love to me.

FEBRUARY 15

Travelling Light

When Jesus sent his seventy-two disciples out to minister, he told them to travel light — no walking stick, no travel bag. There was to be no suitcase for carrying a change of clothes or for stashing away a sandwich. And all of this at a time when there were no laundromats or fast food places! What symbolism. Jesus asked the disciples not to rely on themselves. Their task was a difficult one, but it was to be accomplished by God's power, not theirs. The outcome of their mission was God's problem, not theirs. Could all of this have a personal meaning for us?

People are challenged whenever they offer love and hope to those who sometimes might seem unlovable and hopeless. Those who care for others have to travel light, for they have to rely primarily on God's power rather than their own. And the results of their efforts will finally have to be God's concern rather than theirs. In this sense, travelling light would mean a total trust in God as we offer our care to those who need it.

Travelling light doesn't come easily for me, Lord. I'm tempted to trust too much in my own methods and to be too attached to the outcomes of what I do. We work in partnership,

Lord, but help me to see that you are the senior partner.

FEBRUARY 16

Written in Heaven

When the seventy-two disciples returned from their tour of ministry, they were elated because even the demons were subject to them in Jesus' name. When Jesus saw their elation, he replied,

> "I saw Satan fall like lightning from heaven. Listen! I have given you authority, so that you can walk on snakes and scorpions and overcome all the power of the Enemy, and nothing will hurt you. But don't be glad because the evil spirits obey you; rather be glad because your names are written in heaven" (Lk 10:18–20).

The disciples offered the love of God, and the demons of hate lost out. But according to Jesus, this, great as it was, should not have been the final reason for the disciples' joy. The disciples were invited to find a greater joy in who they were, rather than in what they did. And who were they? People whose names were written in heaven. Jesus told them to be joyful simply because they were his.

Lord, teach me to be joyful simply because I am yours.

46

The Wishes of God

To all of his disciples, Jesus says, "Come, follow me." To what experiences will he lead his followers? What responses will be expected of them? What does it mean to you personally when Jesus says, "Come, follow me"?

Look at the Lord who patiently waits for you to follow, and you will know what he wants from you. God wants your attention and your love.

Look at the people who need your love and your recognition, and you will know what God wants from you. God wants you to care for those who need your caring.

Look at the environment which slowly dies because of human abuse, and you will know what God wants from you. God wants you to treasure what he has made.

It isn't difficult to know what you ask of me, Lord. But to do what you ask, that's another matter.

Mistakes

Twice the audience had asked the tenor to sing a well known aria, and now, they were asking for yet a third repeat.

"Why do you want the same aria three times in a row?" he asked. "Don't you want to hear something else?"

"No," shouted a man in the audience. "Keep on singing it until you get it right."

People who do not learn from their mistakes are doomed to repeat them. The maxim applies to all areas of life. When people notice that their relationships continue to sour and their projects continue to fail, it pays for them to identify the causes. An honest evaluation may show that they themselves are to blame, and if they are, then changes need to be made. If one's mistakes remain the same, so do the results they cause.

Sometimes I've found it easier to blame my mistakes on others rather than on myself. Those were the times when it was difficult for me to change those attitudes and actions in my life that didn't work. Grant me a continuing honesty, Lord, that I might change in myself what needs to be changed.

FEBRUARY 19

Simply Being

When Jesus visited Mary and Martha, Mary sat at his feet and listened while Martha handled the kitchen duties (Lk 10:38–42). While we might have empathized with Martha, it was Mary who received Jesus' approval. How are we to understand this story? What can we learn from it?

Perhaps Jesus was saying to Martha that her life would be incomplete unless she took more time to be quiet and listen. Otherwise, her excessive distractions would cause her to miss what was really important. Maybe our own experience bears this out. When we consistently become too busy, we not only miss God, but also the fullness of our relationships with our families and friends. If we forget the importance of being quietly present to others, we lose sight of who they really are.

Lord, you seem to be saying to me that being is sometimes better than doing. Of course, you know that I'm not fully convinced, but maybe I can learn from my own experience. Help me to spend time being quietly present to you, to my family, and to my friends.

FEBRUARY 20

Becoming Empty

"For whoever wants to save his own life will lose it, but whoever loses his life for my sake will save it."

— Luke 9:24

Jesus taught that no one is filled unless he or she first becomes empty. There is no room for Jesus in the hearts of those who are already filled with themselves.

What is it that keeps you from being more fully open to experience the life-giving presence of Jesus? What do you cling to that keeps you from being free to be filled? And when you discover what it is, will you have the courage to let go?

I'm afraid, Lord, that if I let go of the persons or things I cling to, I may be left with nothing. Strengthen my faith in your promises. Help me to let go and to trust you, that I might be free to experience you and the gift of others more deeply.

Stagnancy

Few things are so uninviting as a stagnant pond. No springs feed it. No outflow cleanses it. Closed in upon itself, it not only develops a disagreeable odor, but it also becomes a breeding place for disease.

People closed in on themselves can become like stagnant ponds. No love comes into them to nourish them. No love comes out of them for the nourishment of others. Living only for themselves, their lives lose the freshness and joy that come from human love and concern for others.

Lord, my fear is that I might slowly become stagnant without fully realizing that this is happening to me. May I be attentive to your Spirit within me, and to the needs of those around me, so that I never close in upon myself.

Caring

In the Good Samaritan story (Lk 10:25–37), the priest and Levite ignore their responsibilities to an injured man desperately in need of help. A Samaritan, a stranger, stops and offers the life-giving assistance denied by the other travelers. The Samaritan appears to be more of a decent human being than the priest and Levite. We pride ourselves on being decent human beings. Why do we sometimes betray our own finer sensibilities and ignore those who need us? Can it be because we have lost touch with our own past sufferings?

Someone who forgets his or her own past sufferings usually has difficulty in relating to the sufferings of others. People out of touch with their own needs and weaknesses may not understand the needs and weaknesses of those around them. A husband who could never understand his wife's sickness finally understood when he himself became sick.

It would seem that most people have experienced some kind of suffering in their lives. It is in the remembrance of one's own suffering and in the awareness of personal weaknesses that compassion for others can take root and grow.

I don't suffer willingly, Lord, but I know that suffering can teach many lessons. May my own suffering teach me to be compassionate to others.

Unconditional Love

Many people become emotionally crippled because they feel unloved, unaccepted, and misunderstood. A part of them dies. How will they be brought back to life?

Those who follow Jesus are called to be life-givers. They are asked to freely give what they have received. And what they have received from God is unconditional love, acceptance, and understanding.

Once we realize the gift of unconditional love and acceptance that God has given us, we are asked to help others realize that this gift has also been given to them. How will they ever understand that if they do not receive love and acceptance from us?

Lord, may my relationships with others reveal something of your own love for them.

Just for You, Lord

Half of the petitions of the Our Father seem to have little to do with our immediate needs. We pray, "Hallowed be your name. Your kingdom come. Your will be done on earth as it is in heaven." Of course, there would be something in it for us if that part of the Our Father were realized, because the world would be a better place to live in. But still, those phrases seem more concerned with God's glory and success than with ourselves. And that is the point. If God were truly a friend, that would be precisely the way we would talk to him. "Here I am, Lord. Right now, I don't want anything. I only pray that your kingdom come, that your will be done, that your name always be revered and held holy. Why? Simply because I love you."

My most joyful moments in prayer have been those in which I've loved you, Lord, simply for who you are.

FEBRUARY 25

Staying Awake

"Be ready for whatever comes, dressed for action and with your lamps lit, like servants who are waiting for their master to come back from a wedding feast. When he comes and knocks, they will open the door for him at once."

— Luke 12:35–36

This invitation to readiness seems to pertain to the future. But is this also an invitation for the present? God comes to us now. God is not content to wait until the end of our lives. Our full response to Jesus' invitation to readiness is to recognize God now, or else we might not recognize him when he appears at the end of our earthly time.

We recognize God in the friendships we enjoy, because they are a reflection of God's love. We recognize God in the world that he has created, because the rivers, trees, streams, and stars all say something about the creator. We recognize God in the strength we get when we cry out to him in times of crisis, for then we see him fulfilling his promise to help us. All of these appearances of God can come at any moment of our lives. We never know when. But we will miss him if we are asleep, if we are not ready to see.

I don't want to miss you today, Lord. Help me to stay awake.

FEBRUARY 26

Journey

God asked Abraham to give up his home and to travel to a place he did not know (Gn 12:1). It was to be a journey of faith and Abraham made it, hoping that God would keep his promises and that the full meaning of the journey would one day be clear. The journey was not without its testings, but neither was it without its rewards. God made him the father of a new people, one from whom the incarnate presence of God would be born.

Our own journey is not unlike the journey of Abraham. We too are asked to accept change with an attitude of faith, not knowing clearly where it will lead. We too have a hope, and our hope is that God will keep the promises made to us in the gospel and that the full meaning of our own journey will one day be clear. And our journey will not be without its testings, but neither will it be without its rewards. God has made us brothers and sisters in a new kingdom, one which will eternally reveal the presence of the incarnate God.

Today is another part of my journey toward you, Lord. May I travel it without fear.

FEBRUARY 27

Only You

You were born to give a certain message to the world, to accomplish a certain task that only you can accomplish. Do you know what it is? Maybe the answer will come more fully if you listen to God in your heart, reflect on your gifts, and realize what it is that others need from you. The greatest personal tragedy would be if your message were never given, and your task never accomplished, for then you would never realize the meaning of your life.

Enlighten me, Lord. Teach me to understand how to give of myself to others and how to determine where it is that I am needed. May I not waste time, Lord, and may I be content with the results of what I do.

FEBRUARY 28

Stewardship

When Jesus chased the moneychangers out of the Temple (Jn 2:13–17), he never rebuked them for being moneychangers, but for going about it in the wrong way. The presence of moneychangers was necessary, so that the foreign coins of travelers could be changed into the acceptable currency of the local area. But Jesus rebuked the money-changers because they allowed their occupation to encroach upon the Temple, and to blind themselves to the presence of God. He rebuked them because they used their occupations simply for their own selfish ends.

What would Jesus have to tell us about the way we carry out our occupations? What would he have to say to us about the way we use money?

Whatever I have comes from you, Lord, to be used according to the dictates of wisdom and love. Grant me the insight to do this so that I might live in harmony with your will.

FEBRUARY 29

An Extra Day

Leap year! Some people think that the addition of this day really gives them more time. But whether or not this day is added to the calendar, their life span remains the same. The measuring of time is an invention of human beings. Living it well is an action of saints.

Let us, just for a moment, put aside our watches, calendars, and appointment books. Let us not ask how much we can cram into our artificial measurements of time but rather how well we live in the time that is being given to us.

I don't ask for a long life, Lord, but rather for the strength to live well in the time that I have.

MARCH 1

Divisions

"Do not think that I have come to bring peace to the world. No, I did not come to bring peace, but a sword."

— Matthew 10:34

Throughout the gospel, the words of Jesus are often words of peace and reconciliation. We long for that part of his mission to be realized, but sometimes we are unprepared for his warnings about division. Divisions will be a result of Jesus' mission. We may have already experienced this.

People who are deeply religious sometimes come to be resented in their families and communities. A person deeply in love with God attracts some and repels others. Jesus himself was not immune to this phenomenon. And on a communal level, we ourselves may find it hard to accept the religious expressions of others when they do not conform to our preconceived ideas. In a pluralistic church, the experience of division is sometimes as real as the experience of peace.

Yes, Lord, I must admit that I experience the divisions that you warned about. I don't ask that others totally conform to my vision of things. I do ask that I might have the love to accept those who honestly follow what they think is right.

MARCH 2

Wholeness

"I do not understand what I do; for I don't do what I would like to do, but instead I do what I hate."

— Romans 7:15

Perhaps you remember the story of Dr. Jekyll and Mr. Hyde. Jekyll, the good personality, and Hyde, the deficient personality, were both in the same individual. In spite of Jekyll's best intentions, Hyde sometimes took over in terrible ways that Jekyll did not want. The story parallels the experience that seems imbedded in the quote from Romans. Most likely, it also parallels our own experience. We notice a split within ourselves. Two opposite parts of us never quite come together and it seems to us that we are helpless to do much about it. What is the answer?

"What an unhappy man I am! Who will rescue me from this body that is taking me to death? Thanks be to God, who does this through our Lord Jesus Christ!" (Rom 7:24–25). For Paul, it is the power of Jesus that leads us back to wholeness. The growth toward wholeness begins when we rely on the healing power of God which is given to those who ask. The process is a gradual one, but God is patient. And we must be patient too.

The things I don't want to do, I do. I feel the split within myself, Lord. Heal the division within me, but teach me to be patient with the healing process, as you yourself are patient.

MARCH 3

The Narrow Gate

"Go in through the narrow gate, because the gate to hell is wide and the road that leads to it is easy, and there are many who travel it. But the gate to life is narrow and the way that leads to it is hard, and there are few people who find it."

— Matthew 7:13–14

Jesus seems to be saying that it is not easy to find life. One has to go through the narrow gate. Doing good to someone who hates you is to go through the narrow gate. To accept without bitterness the suffering that is a part of life is to enter through the narrow gate. To love those who seem unlovable, to

59

serve others at some expense to yourself — all this is to go through the narrow gate.

Jesus invites us to make choices for love in our daily lives that finally lead to the fullness of life with Christ in heaven. We need to narrow our egos so that we can respond to the broader needs of those around us. That seems to be the narrow path that broadens out into the completeness of life now, and in the agelessness to come.

I admit to you that the narrow gate sometimes seems constricting, Lord. Give me the love to experience that the narrow gate leads to joy.

MARCH 4

Remembrance

Remember all the gifts of life that God has given to you in the past: the touch of God in your life, the presence of those who have loved you, the material things that brought you joy. Recall them in detail. Remembrance of all this refreshes the present moment and brings confidence in those moments that seem to lack the promise of hope.

Faith weakens when our gratitude dies. How many gifts of life have you received and forgotten?

Let me not forget all that I have received, Lord, for you have touched my life in many ways. Of course, the gifts of your love are partly different now from what they were in the past, but I want to recall my entire life so that I can understand how you were present in it, even in the sufferings. I know you were with me in the past. I believe that you are with me in the present. I believe that you will be with me in the future.

MARCH 5

Brokenness

It is essential for us to admit our brokenness, or else we might think that we are whole. That would be a delusion. An honest evaluation of ourselves reveals much brokenness, and the Bible repeats what we already know about ourselves. How will we open to the possibility of growth into wholeness? By admitting that we are broken.

Do you have the courage to take an inventory of yourself, and to acknowledge those areas of your life where there is brokenness? Through your honest admission, you will open yourself to God's healing. What was dead in you will be brought to life.

Open my eyes, Lord, that I may see my brokenness. Open my heart, that I might be healed.

MARCH 6

Temptation

Jesus returned from the Jordan full of the Holy Spirit and was led by the Spirit into the desert, where he was tempted by the Devil for forty days. In all that time he ate nothing, so that he was hungry when it was over. The

Devil said to him, "If you are God's Son, order this stone to turn into bread." But Jesus answered, "The scripture says, 'Man cannot live on bread alone.'"

— Luke 4:1–4

Why should this be regarded as a temptation? After forty days of fasting, eating bread would seem to be an acceptable activity, even if the bread had to be changed from stone. Jesus had the power to perform this miracle, but it seems that his power was to be used for the benefit of others, rather than for himself. Perhaps this is one of the lessons for us in Jesus' refusal to change stone into bread.

How do we use our personal gifts, talents, and our material possessions? Are these given to us only for ourselves? Do we ever use them to enrich the lives of others? To use our gifts, talents, and possessions without regard to others is to waste what we have been given.

I am often tempted to use my gifts for my own pleasure and to forget that your gifts to me are meant to be shared. Lord, may I not yield to this temptation.

MARCH 7

Fidelity

Then the Devil took him up and showed him in a second all the kingdoms of the world. "I will give you all this power and all this wealth," the Devil told him. "It has

all been handed over to me, and I can give
it to anyone I choose. All this will be yours,
then, if you worship me." Jesus answered,
"The scripture says, 'Worship the Lord your
God and serve only him!' "

— Luke 4:5–8

Life is a series of choices in which we set our priorities. Fidelity to God's love and to God's plan is the
top priority for those who love God. Temptation in
the gospel is not so much an inducement to sin as
it is a test that proves our fidelity to God. Where
are we tempted to be unfaithful? When those times
come, be prepared. The more we are aware of God's
power and presence in our lives, the more we can
meet the test of fidelity when we are challenged.

*It is your power within me that enables me to
be faithful. Lord, may I always be faithful to
you.*

MARCH 8

Testing God

Then the Devil took him to Jerusalem and
set him on the highest point of the Temple, and said to him, "If you are God's
Son, throw yourself down from here. For
the scripture says, 'God will order his an-
gels to take good care of you.' It also says,
'They will hold you up with their hands so
that not even your feet will be hurt on the

stones.' " But Jesus answered, "The scripture says, 'Do not put the Lord your God to the test.' "

— Luke 4:9–12

How do we put God to the test? We test God whenever we expect the Lord to do for us what we are able to do for ourselves. It is true that God makes all our good works possible, and that without God, we can do nothing. But when we pray and then refuse to work in partnership with God, then we put the Lord to the test.

God will not do for us what we can do for ourselves. Peace and justice are the works of God, but they will not be realized in our midst unless they become our works too. To presume otherwise is to test God.

I don't intentionally put you to the test, Lord, but what am I to say about my callousness toward others? Do I presume that you will take care of others when I do so little to meet their needs?

MARCH 9

The Butterfly

A caterpillar may not seem like one of God's most beautiful creatures, but nature slowly changes it until it finally becomes what it is meant to be — a butterfly. This new creature no longer crawls; it flies. It no longer chews on leaves; it sips sweet tasting nectar. The caterpillar has not been destroyed;

it has been transformed and it takes on a new kind of life.

The butterfly is an apt symbol of the resurrection. It symbolizes that we will not be destroyed in death, but transformed and given a new life. The transformation already begins in this life as we die to selfishness and grow into love. And if we choose the beginnings of this transformation now, God will complete it through our death and resurrection into a new life that will be everlasting. This is the promise of Jesus.

Lord, may I experience something of the resurrection now through a death to selfishness and a rebirth into love.

MARCH 10

Surrender

Our most courageous and faith-filled act happens whenever we surrender to the will of God. It is in this act of trust and love that we finally find our peace. But there is within us an animosity to parts of life that keeps us from making this act of trust and love. We rebel against the experience of aging, the death of someone we love, sickness, and the other crosses that are a part of life. Unless we learn to accept what we cannot change, how can we surrender to what must be, to the God who brings good out of evil?

I know that you don't cause suffering, Lord, but I do know that you permit it, and that you shared in our sufferings. The sufferings that I

*can't change I will accept, even though I won't
always understand why they have to be. Help
me to walk with you even when the walk is
painful, to accept your will when it seems to
differ from my own.*

MARCH 11

Giving

"When you give a lunch or a dinner, do not
invite your friends or your brothers or your
relatives or your rich neighbors — for they
will invite you back, and in this way you
will be paid for what you did. When you
give a feast, invite the poor, the crippled, the
lame, and the blind; and you will be blessed,
because they are not able to pay you back.
God will repay you on the day the good
people rise from death."

— Luke 14:12–14

Jesus' advice runs counter to immediate self-
interest, but in the long run, his advice serves a
genuine personal good. People who give just for
the sake of giving come to understand what love
means, and in this understanding, they find their
joy. If we never experience that kind of joy, we
never come to know who we are, or what our life
means, or who God is.

*I admit, Lord, that much of what I do is done
more out of self-interest than out of genuine
love. Change my selfishness through your*

power, that I might love and serve without the thought of gaining something for myself.

MARCH 12

Heroic Love

Jesus frequently associated with sinners, tax collectors, and others who were not considered to be very lovable. In Jesus, God showed us what divine love was really like.

Many times in the gospel, we are asked to love those who are seemingly unlovable to us, and to forgive those who have hurt us. If we refuse these experiences, we cannot know what God is like.

Every day, we are in need of forgiveness, and even when we fail to admit our need, God's love never stops penetrating us. As God is toward us, so we are asked to be toward others. When we do what God does, loving as he loves, then we become like him, and we come to experience his peace.

I'm thinking of the people whom I find hard to love and to forgive. I can never love them, Lord, unless I realize that you make it possible. God, I want to love as you love. Otherwise, I will never be one with you.

MARCH 13

The Measure of Success

How successful are you? Some people try to figure out the answer by checking their bank accounts.

Others examine the amount of power they have or the prestige they enjoy in their organizations and communities. But all of these things eventually pass away. And when they are all gone, as they most certainly will be when you breathe out your last breath, the question can be asked again: how successful are you? The only true measure of success then will be the measure of love with which you have lived your life.

Lord, your ideas of human success are different from most people's ideas. I will be successful to the extent that I do in my life what you did in yours. Help me to reflect on this, that I might see more clearly what this means in the particular circumstances of my life.

MARCH 14

Gratitude

Confucius said, "When you see a noble man, try to equal him. When you see an evil man, examine yourself thoroughly." Did he want to say that the possibilities of evil are within us, and that we are sometimes unaware of them? Do we even understand the value of those in our lives who have enabled us to do good and avoid evil? If we have not succumbed to the possibilities of evil within us, we have the grace of God to thank, along with the favorable circumstances of our own lives. Yes, our free will entered in too. But how much we owe to God and to those who have loved us for helping us to make the good choices we have made.

Can you think of concrete circumstances in your life when this has been true?

Lord, I examine my life with gratitude, but even when I try to recall my past, I can never be fully aware of how much I have received from you and from those who have loved me. Without your goodness and the goodness of others to help me, how would my own life have been good? Even so, Lord, I am aware of my possibilities for evil, and of my failures. Guide me in the ways of your path.

MARCH 15

Availability

Jesus took Peter and two other disciples into the garden of Gethsemane that he might find support from them in the midst of his suffering. But they fell asleep. According to Luke, they fell asleep because they were exhausted with their own grief (Lk 22:45). Whatever the full causes of their sleepiness might have been, they were not available to Jesus when he needed them.

Our own preoccupations, no matter how legitimate, sometimes cause us to center our attention excessively on ourselves. What is it in our own lives that keeps us from responding to those who need our presence? In allowing ourselves to be overwhelmed by our own preoccupations, do we make ourselves unavailable to others?

"Could you not stay awake with me for even an hour?" Is this question that you asked your

*apostles also addressed to me, Jesus? When-
ever I sleep through the cries of the needy, your
question challenges me.*

MARCH 16

Simplicity

"I assure you that whoever does not receive
the Kingdom of God like a child will never
enter it."

— Mark 10:15

Those who do not take the workings of their minds
too seriously have a better chance of becoming like
a child than those who do. Intellectual achievement
is a great gift; realizing the limits of intellectual
achievement is an even greater gift. Sometimes the
workings of our logical minds keep us from the
faith and the intuitive wonder that children experience. They have the ability to be awed and charmed
by life, while adults often rationalize the charm out
of life. What a gift to be both an analytical adult
and a trusting child at the same time.

*Jesus, how many times I have been childish
rather than child-like. Teach me the fact that
truth can never be fully grasped by human
logic. Help me to recapture the experience of
simple faith and intuitive wonder that can open
to me another dimension of who you are.*

MARCH 17

Thoughts

It is not just our exterior actions, but also our interior thoughts that determine who we are before God and before our fellow human beings (Mt 5:21–22; 27–28). Inner attitudes affect our exterior relationships in subtle ways. Hatred in the heart can color our actions just as much as hatred that is explicitly expressed. It is the same with unbridled sexual thoughts and desires. Even when the thoughts are not acted upon, they begin to change the way we react to others, as well as the way we spend our mental energies.

Thoughts are powerful realities, and that is why Jesus shows a concern about them. We become our thoughts, and what we are eventually radiates toward others.

Heal me at the core of my being, Jesus, that my thoughts may be wholesome and bring joy to others and to myself.

MARCH 18

Answered Prayers

How would you feel if every one of your prayers were always answered as you wished? Imagine an ongoing experience in which God's response to you always harmonized with your deepest desires. How would you ever get to a state of being where such harmony would seem normal?

Certainly this would never happen through your attempts to bend God's will to your own. It could happen, though, if you learned to think and love as God does. The more you would come to know God, the more you would understand how to pray. And the more you understood how to pray, the more your prayer would be in harmony with God's will. And, in praying in harmony with God's will, you could be certain that your prayers would be answered as you intended.

If I were truly in harmony with you, Lord, I would know how to pray, for your Spirit would be praying within me. Teach me how to be one in mind and heart with you, that our wills might be the same.

MARCH 19

Humor

Is there anyone who can survive life without a sense of humor? Sometimes there is a funny side to the minor fiascos and inconveniences of our lives. We can discover that side if we are sufficiently optimistic and creative.

Without a sense of humor, we lose a sense of perspective. Life's difficulties seem heavier than they really are. A sense of humor is a potential within ourselves that most of us are capable of developing. It may involve quite a change in the way we look at things, but it helps us to avoid making crosses where God never intended them to be.

Humor is one of your gifts, Lord, an energy-saver that frees me from being drained by my

*minor misfortunes. Teach me to laugh at the
small afflictions and mishaps of my life, and
then to move on, so that I can avoid becoming
entrapped by joylessness and self-pity.*

MARCH 20

Time

Do you sometimes regret the hatreds in your life
that have not been healed, or the love in your relationships that has remained unspoken? Live this
day as if it were your last. We think we have so
much time, and so a lot of what we want to do
is left undone. If you knew that you had no more
time, what would you do today for someone you
love? What would you do for God? What would
you do for yourself?

*I procrastinate, Lord. I take time for granted
and waste so much of it. Now I want to use
my time wisely, so that my life will not be a
waste. Today, where there is love to be given,
I will give it. Where there is something to be
done for others, I will do it. Where there is a
task to be completed, I will finish it.*

MARCH 21

Spring

Spring, the promise of new life; Easter, the promise
of our resurrection! Both events speak to us of the
present, and both contain the seeds of the future.

Spring looks to the fullness of growth and harvest, and Easter looks to the fullness of our rebirth at the end of time.

We live in the present, and at the same time, we are drawn toward the future. The wise person knows how to live fully with his or her eyes on both, for the promises of Jesus are not only about the present time, but also about the agelessness to come.

Thank you, Lord, for the spring, and for all your signs and promises that touch both time and eternity. You are with me in this present moment, but you will also bring me to the fullness of life in the age to come. These promises are magnificent, Lord, but my appreciation of them is dull. Deepen my appreciation and sharpen my love.

M A R C H 22

Beginnings

How this day turns out depends, in part, on how it begins. Begin your day with an attitude of joyful anticipation, and you reap the reward of your own state of mind. Begin it with disgust or reluctance, and your state of mind will pursue you as the hours unfold. You set the tone of your day by the way you welcome it.

Each day is a gift of God to us, but sometimes the gift comes wrapped in somber colors. We may wake up with pain, or with the knowledge that we face a difficult or disagreeable task. Trusting that

74

God is with us can give us the courage we need. Looking forward to something pleasant can lessen the difficulties we have to face. Learning to believe in ourselves can calm the fears we feel. However we choose to begin this day, we do have the power to determine, to some extent, what this day will be like.

You have given me this day, Lord, and I want to receive it with as joyful a heart as I can. I have the power to make it more beautiful. I have the power to lessen its pains. I have the power to rediscover its joys. May I live this day as you would have me live it.

MARCH 23

Mistakes

People often find it difficult to admit their mistakes. That may be because they have difficulty in believing that they are unconditionally loved and accepted.

We can freely admit our mistakes before God, because God's unconditional love offers us forgiveness whenever we are willing to receive it. How hard it is to understand this, because our love is so different from God's love. When we accept God's love in all of its awesome fidelity, we are enabled to admit who we are, because, whoever we are, we are always loved.

Knowing that God loves us as he does, we are able to take risks with others. Even if they reject us, there is always Someone who accepts us for what we are, mistakes and all.

I freely admit to you all that I am, Lord, my mistakes as well as my strengths. I sometimes doubt that you love me as much as you say, but I don't really want to doubt your word. I want to believe with all the belief that your word deserves.

MARCH 24

Forging Ahead

Sometimes we get stuck in attitudes that we need to leave behind. If we are dissatisfied with our lives, it may be that we are holding on to something that is no longer satisfying, something we need to die to so that we can be reborn to something deeper and more mature. This is one of the meanings of losing our lives that we might find them. It is one of the meanings of the cross. The process of letting go is a painful experience, but it leads to maturity, to a new experience of something deeper in life. We have to ask what this process means for us at this point in our lives. What is it that we need to grow out of, or grow up to?

I'm never too old to grow up, Lord, but I'm often afraid to let go of relationships and things that no longer satisfy. Sometimes a vague dissatisfaction in life urges me to let go, and to go onward, but I either ignore the message or miss its point. I ask for the gifts of courage and wisdom.

The Request

What an awesome request! God asks Mary through a messenger if she would be willing to bear his Son (Lk 1:26–38). Mary's acceptance became the gateway for Jesus' entry into our human existence. Her "yes" brought Jesus to each one of us who is willing to accept him. And when we say our "yes" to Jesus, we continue the process of bringing him to others. Whenever we make a place for Jesus within ourselves and allow him to change our lives, then in a very real way we also bring him to others.

The request made of Mary is also made to us. We are asked to be carriers of Jesus, even though we do the carrying in vessels of clay. In fact, that is what makes the carrying all the more magnificent. And if we carry him with energetic enthusiasm, then perhaps others will catch the fire.

You are within me, Lord. You tell me that in many different ways in the Bible. I accept you willingly. May I radiate your presence and your strength to others whom I meet this day.

Idiosyncrasies

Most idiosyncrasies seem harmless, but some lead to spiritual growth, while others lead to spiritual decay. A chaste person in our society might seem "out-of-sync," but his or her idiosyncrasy leads to spiritual growth and health. A person who is not "out to get his or hers" may seem out of step with society, but he or she is on the way to love. But there are people out of step in an opposite sense, out of step, for example, with the love they receive from their families and communities. Their idiosyncrasies lead away from spiritual health.

Perhaps many of our own idiosyncrasies are harmless. But do some of them lead us away from what we really want to be? On the other hand, if we are out of step with the inauthentic directions of society, are we embarrassed, or do we count ourselves blest?

Speak to me about my idiosyncrasies, Lord. They are a part of me. Which of them keep me from you? Which ones are truly gifts?

MARCH 27

Reconciliation

When people find a chasm separating them, prayer is a bridge that can bring them together. It may be that only one of the people involved will have sufficient self-forgetfulness to pray for the healing of the rift. But the prayer of only one person can still be a healing power. No one knows exactly how this works, but Jesus said that if we bring a gift to the altar and remember that we are at odds with someone, we should first be reconciled and then offer the gift (Mt 5:23–24). To make the attempt is essential, but even if the offer of reconciliation is refused, prayer does reconcile the heart of the pray-er. And our own hearts are the only ones over which we have any control.

There were times when I found it too difficult to pray for those who had hurt me. For those times, I am sorry, Lord. May I not only pray for those who have hurt me, but may I seek reconciliation in any way I can for the sake of peace.

MARCH 28

Light

"You are like light for the whole world. A city built on a hill cannot be hid. No one lights a lamp and puts it under a bowl; instead he puts it on the lampstand, where it gives light for everyone in the house. In the same way your light must shine before people, so that they will see the good things you do and praise your Father in heaven."

— Matthew 5:14–16

It is God who enables us to be light to others. The power is his. That is why it is no small thing for us to be like light for others. We only receive what we have been given, and what we have been given comes from the source of all light. Jesus tells us that the light we have received must shine before others. In this way, what we do to spread light is finally for the glory of God.

To bring light to others is to bring them the truth that they are loved and valued. If we show that to others and they believe it, then they too are enabled to become light-bearers. It is God's will that the light of his truth and love should envelop the world. His will is done whenever someone realizes that the light is within and that it is meant to be shared.

I've never thought of myself as a light for others, Lord, but that is what you have called me to be. Thank you for your power within me which is my light. May it radiate from me for the good of others.

MARCH 29

Friends

"I do not call you servants any longer, because a servant does not know what his master is doing. Instead, I call you friends, because I have told you everything I heard from my Father."

— John 15:15

Jesus calls us his friends. The term "friend" has many different meanings. What does this term mean for you?

A friend is someone who encourages us and builds us up, someone who acknowledges our presence instead of ignoring us. A friend believes the best about our potential, even while being aware of our failures. A friend accepts us as we are and would do anything in his or her power to respond to our legitimate needs. If all of this is what it means to be a friend, then Jesus certainly is a friend to us.

Of course, one could say much more about friendship, and whatever could be said would describe what Jesus is for us. How do you understand the meaning of friendship, and how is that meaning embodied in Jesus' relationship with you?

If I really believed that your love were as personal as you say, Lord, I would see you as a friend beyond all others. I want to grow toward this realization, but I have a long way to go. Sharpen my insights, and deepen my faith.

M A R C H 30

Spiritual Gifts

St. Paul tells us that there are different spiritual gifts given to each of us for the building up of the community of God (1 Cor 12:11–14). These gifts are outpourings of the goodness of God upon his people. What a tragedy if we never discover what our gifts are, or if we sell ourselves short by preferring others' talents to those of our own.

Our lives are for a purpose, and there are those whose lives we are meant to touch. Just as there is someone who has brought life and love to us, so there is someone who, unknowingly perhaps, awaits these from us. We have been given our own spiritual talents as gifts of the Spirit that we might heal and enrich the lives of others. This is God's doing. He invites our cooperation that his work might be completed.

Lord, preserve me from thinking that I have nothing to give to others, for that would

81

dishonor your gifts within me and be a waste of who I am. Teach me the truth about myself, and help me to see the giftedness that I either miss or deny.

MARCH 31

Endurance

Some difficulties and sufferings cannot be changed or healed no matter what we do. In spite of our best efforts, some attempts at reconciliation will be refused, occasionally our plans will go awry, and some of our infirmities will remain without cure. We are not always in control of these things. What we can do is to ask for the power to accept the things we cannot change. But is there any hope in that?

St. Paul said that the sufferings of this life could never be compared to the glory that is to come (Rom 8:18). Our endurance is only a temporary necessity, because our unavoidable sufferings borne with love eventually give rise to the peace and freedom of the resurrection, where every tear is wiped away. And in the present moment, patient endurance plants the seed of peace that germinates even now.

I know that my rebellion against the things I cannot change destroys my peace. Help me to accept what I cannot change, that I might bring peace to myself and to others. Above all, may I continue to trust in you and hope in your promises.

APRIL

APRIL 1

Fools

Be on guard. Somebody may try to fool you today. The term "fool" can have many different meanings. An easily outwitted person is sometimes, unkindly of course, called a fool. People who disagree with us might seem to be fools to us. Those whom the world does not recognize as its own will sometimes be called fools. Their standards are either unintelligible to the world at large, or a reproach to the consciences of those who do not share them. Perhaps being a fool in this sense is not such a bad thing.

St. Paul wrote that he and the apostles were fools on Christ's account (1 Cor 4:10). The sufferings they endured for God might have seemed foolish to some, but to Paul and the apostles, it would have seemed foolish to have acted otherwise. A selfless lifestyle might indeed appear foolish to those who cannot understand this kind of love, but that was the way of Jesus. And as St. Paul wrote, "For what seems to be God's foolishness is wiser than human wisdom, and what seems to be God's weakness is stronger than human strength" (1 Cor 1:25).

Do you call me to be a fool for you, Jesus? If I were really to put aside selfish concerns and follow you with complete fidelity, I might be regarded as foolish by some. I hope I would have the courage not to care about what others think. I ask that I may always care about what you think. May I never appear foolish in your eyes.

APRIL 2

Creativity

The four men who brought the paralytic to Jesus were unable to bring him through the front door because of the huge crowd that had gathered there. And so they made a hole in the roof over the spot where Jesus was, and they lowered the paralytic through it. Jesus marvelled at their faith and cured the paralytic, forgiving his sins and sending him home (Mk 2:1–12).

What if the four men had seen the crowd around the house, and then given up their enterprise as being impossible to accomplish? Instead, they had the creative insight to work around the obstacle, to find another way into the house. Their creative faith was rewarded. Because of their perseverance, the paralytic walked again.

When we run into problems with ourselves and with others, or when there seem to be obstacles in our path to God, are we able to be creative in dealing with them? Through quiet prayer, or maybe through consultation with a friend, what different approaches might be discovered? If the front door approach does not work, maybe we could try the roof. One thing is sure. People open to alternative, creative approaches in dealing with obstacles are more likely to succeed than those who are closed.

I want to learn from this story of the paralytic, Lord. Many times in my life, I've lacked the faith to deal with the obstacles of my life creatively. Teach me what a more creative faith might mean for me. May I have the patience to be silent and to reflect.

APRIL 3

Coming to Life

"I am the resurrection and the life."
— John 11:25

The resurrection is the wholeness of life that is God's gift to us. Are we growing toward this wholeness? Trust in Jesus liberates us from the anxieties, fears, and resentments that rob us of life by keeping us fragmented and unfree.

Jesus came that we might have the fullness of life. That is God's deepest desire for all human beings. Having life to the full would be a life in which pettiness, selfishness, resentment, and fear are put to death through the power of Jesus living within us. We have this power because Jesus died and rose. His resurrection is the event that enables us to rise from whatever it is in our lives that keeps us from living fully. Our growth toward wholeness is his gift to us, so that we might have life now, and have it to the full. What is it that keeps us from accepting this gift?

Choosing a way of life that leads toward whole-ness seems like a reasonable action, Lord, but I often choose paths that lead away from it. Jesus, you know me. You understand my weakness. By your cross and resurrection, may I choose the way of love that leads to fullness of life, and avoid whatever leads away from it.

APRIL 4

The Vine

"I am the vine, and you are the branches. Whoever remains in me, and I in him, will bear much fruit; for you can do nothing without me."

— John 15:5

So much failure comes from our attempts to live without God. We put our lives into his hands, and then we panic and try to run them by ourselves. Trust is not an attitude that comes easily to most of us. We seem to feel uncomfortable if we are not in total control, calling all the shots. Life rarely gives us that luxury, though. By ourselves, we never succeed in controlling very much at all. Trusting in God's power, we could decide to be content doing what we can, and leaving the results to him.

Whatever successes we have in life are all gifts of God, for his guidance as well as our talents are his gifts. What is it in our lives that we have not received? As the vine fructifies the branch, so are our lives fructified by the power of God, which enables us to be the best of what we can be. The branches can trust the vine.

Jesus, I want to remain in your presence. I put my life into your hands. Deepen my trust, especially when my path seems to lead into darkness. May I never separate myself from the power of your presence, for separated from you, my strength and my talents cannot bear fruit.

APRIL 5

Breaking Out

Remember a time in your past when you broke out of your routine and did something different. The experience was refreshing, and you wondered why you had not done something like that before. You know in theory that breaking out of routine can be life-giving and bring new experiences of consciousness, but have you tried to break out recently? Have you been able to let go of your daily pattern and open yourself to something different, or even take a little time to relax?

How many enjoyable and worthwhile experiences have never seen the light of day because of routine? If you think about this and feel regret, then take the time to be with a friend, or to do something that you find enjoyable. Not only would this sharpen your zest for life, but it would also improve the quality of those things you do as part of your daily routine.

I apologize to you, Lord, for missing so much of the beauty that could have been a part of my life. May I have the wisdom to rearrange my priorities and to expand my awareness of the possibilities in front of me.

APRIL 6

I Didn't Recognize Him

John the Baptizer's ministry was to point out Jesus to his contemporaries, but as John admitted twice, "I still did not know that he was the one..." (Jn 1:33). Perhaps the problem is common to many of us. Those of us who call ourselves Jesus' followers sometimes go through much of our lives somewhat unsure of his presence, unaware of what we could be if we would open our lives to him.

How will you come to recognize God? The recognition comes when you decide to spend quiet time with him in prayer. In opening your thoughts and desires to God and listening to his response, you come to know who he is. It is hard to explain what happens when this is done, but insights come through the process of quiet communication with God that otherwise are missed. These insights will be personal. They will be your own. You will come to know more deeply that you are loved, and you will recognize the one who loves you.

You will also come to recognize him in the caring that you give and receive from others. For then you will be doing what God does. You will become more like God, and in becoming more like him, you will recognize him for who he is.

Through much of my life, I have never really recognized you, Lord. Give me a burning desire to want to know you, to recognize you in the quiet moments I spend with you, and in the caring that I give and receive from others.

APRIL 7

Light

"The people who live in darkness will see a great light. On those who live in the dark land of death the light will shine."

— Matthew 4:16

The gospel challenges us to ask ourselves if we have seen the light. What kind of light did God send us through Jesus?

Before Jesus came, it was not clear to what extent God loved us. But on the evening before he died, Jesus washed his disciples' feet, giving them a service that was done at that time by slaves. God washed the feet of human beings. Then Jesus proceeded to call his disciples "friends," because he had shared his life, his inmost thoughts with them. He said that he would not leave them orphans, that he would always be with them. The next day, he died on the cross, loving the very people who had rejected him and taken his life. Then he rose, having told his disciples that they were meant to share his life into eternity.

This was the way in which God revealed himself to human beings. The revelation was a great light given to people who had been in darkness, for no one had ever imagined that God would be anything like this.

Jesus, the light of what you are has given me hope and made me new. Thank you for this light. May I never again walk in the darkness of being unconscious of you.

APRIL 8

Poor in Spirit

"Happy are those who know they are spiritually poor; the Kingdom of heaven belongs to them!"

— Matthew 5:3

Most of the first Christians came from what sociologists today would call the lower class. They were materially quite poor and needy, ready for a message of salvation. When the message of Jesus reached them, it fell on fertile soil. We may not be quite so materially needy as many of the first Christians, or as many of the Christians today in third world countries. Do our possessions and comforts keep us from hearing and accepting Jesus' presence? Jesus said that the poor in spirit would have the kingdom. What would it mean to be poor in spirit, so that we might be able to accept what he offers us?

Perhaps poverty of spirit would mean the realization that none of our comforts or possessions ultimately satisfies us. That realization would free us from addiction to our comforts and from the amassing of possessions. The resulting freedom would enable us to be more open to the kingdom of God and to the needs of others.

Poverty of spirit could mean the sharing of our time, possessions, and comforts with others. It could mean an expansion of love and giving which, according to Jesus, finally brings the only true experience of joy. But to receive that joy, the joy of the kingdom, we would have to be sharing people, loving, detached, poor in spirit.

Jesus, help me to achieve the freedom that belongs to those who are detached, to the poor in spirit. Give me a hunger for your kingdom, for the love that alone can bring me joy. May I use my time and possessions with a love for you and for others.

APRIL 9

Scars and Shadows

Somewhere in the lives of all of us there were needs that were not met, love that was not given at a time we needed it, acceptance that was denied. These hurts may still exist as scars or shadows on our personalities. Even if we did not have these scars and shadows in ourselves, we would still have to deal with them in others. This is one reason why human relationships can be so difficult. Many of us are among the "walking wounded," people who have to cope daily with psychological and spiritual difficulties that linger from the past and affect the present.

If we want to offer hope and healing to one another, the offer can only be made with compassion and understanding. These attitudes do not come naturally to us. We have to want them, pray for them, and practice them. Prayer helps us to change ourselves, to be compassionate, and to accept what cannot be changed in others. Sometimes, our prayers even help others to change.

No one escapes the effects of the scars left on them by life. Compassionate understanding can heal those effects for all who seek wholeness.

You showed me the meaning of compassion, Lord, by your forgiveness of my malice and culpable ignorance. What I have received from you, may I have the strength to give to others, so that I might help create an atmosphere of hope and healing among those who need it.

APRIL 10

Lightening the Burden

What most people yearn for is not someone to solve their problems, but someone to listen to them. They long to be accepted and understood, to know that someone cares about them and is willing to walk with them through at least a part of their difficult life journey. Someone who does that for another offers a very great service. Listening lightens the burden for others and offers a space where healing can occur.

What about our own burdens? Even though we may prefer to carry our burdens in silence, we have as much need for a caring listener as anybody else. Sometimes important insights come to us when we allow ourselves to talk out our problems. And who could not benefit from the acceptance and encouragement that comes from a listener who cares about us? We can find many excuses to avoid talking about our life burdens, but relief is far more likely to come when we stop carrying our burdens in solitary silence.

You shared your burdens with your apostles, Jesus, especially on the night before you died. Help me to follow you in this act of humility so that my own burdens may be lightened. May I find someone trustworthy, and may I be a trustworthy listener for others.

APRIL 11

Accepting Limitations

"But some seeds fell in good soil, and the plants bore grain: some had one hundred grains, others sixty, and others thirty."

— Matthew 13:8

In the parable about the sower, Jesus speaks of seeds that, for various reasons, never grow to bear grain. But the seeds that do eventually mature and bear grain, do so with varying degrees of productivity. While some are capable of producing a hundred-fold, the capacity of others is much less. And yet, they are still successful, because they produced as much as they could.

This is a part of the parable's message that often fails to get our attention. The parable is not only about the seeds that fail to mature, but also about the seeds that bear grain in different amounts. Those of us who do our best can be happy with our results, even though the results are not perfect. If someone gets a "C" on an exam, and that represents his or her best, then that "C" is a cause for celebration. And that is true for all the rest of the "C's" of human life. God rejoices in what we offer him, no matter how it turns out, so long as the effort is truly our best.

So long as I am doing my best, Lord, I'll be content with the talents I have, and thankful for the results that I achieve. Teach me to accept myself as I am, to be at peace with what I am able to do, and to stop comparing myself to others.

APRIL 12

Roots

When we talk about our roots, we usually refer to our racial or ethnic backgrounds. Such roots say something about who we are, but they do not define us on our deepest level. On the deepest level, the roots of all of us are the same; they are in God. Each one of us can trace his or her roots back to the one who gave everyone the gift of life and the power to love.

The record of these roots is in the Bible. It tells us that we were created by God in his image and that we are sustained by his love. Because of our common heritage, we are all brothers and sisters, joined together by a sharing of the divine life that lives within each of us and makes us one. Such is our dignity, a dignity that flows from our roots in God. Nothing more profound than this can be said about us.

Without being rooted in you, I could never be myself, Lord. I thank you for the full gift of who I am, for the gift of your life that beats within my heart and enables me to love. You are the source of my meaning, the goal of my life.

APRIL 13

Hopelessness

Perhaps Jesus' disciples never felt such hopelessness as they did when they watched him dying on the cross. All of their hopes seemed to be snatched away by this dark, terrible moment. Did they forget Jesus' predictions? Did they fail to remember his promises? It took them a while to grasp the full significance of Jesus' passion, death, and resurrection, for the reality of it seemed too good to be true, too magnificent to be possible.

The triumph of Jesus blossomed out of a situation that seemed, from a human point of view, to be hopeless. As the disciples watched Jesus hanging on the cross, all hopes for the future must have appeared bleak. And yet this bleakness was changed by the power of God into the brightness of the resurrection, a fulfillment for Jesus and a new hope for us. None of this came about through human ingenuity. It was a sheer gift of God.

God has a unique way of dealing with the seemingly hopeless moments of our lives. God has the power to bring healing and new life from our hopeless situations, in ways and in times that we least expect. Do we have the faith to believe that God's love and compassion can bring healing and light from the dark moments of our lives?

Lord, in my seemingly hopeless moments, I've been tempted to doubt that light would ever return to my life. And yet, as I look back, I can see the many ways your love has touched me in my darkness and brought healing and new life to me. Teach me to look at you, my risen Lord, and to believe in your love, your presence, and your power.

APRIL 14

Why Me?

The call of God in human life is not always received with joy. Some of the Old Testament prophets were reluctant hearers of God's call and perhaps wondered why they were the ones who had to be singled out. The rich man heard Jesus' invitation to leave his riches and follow him, and he turned away with sadness (Mk 10:17–25). The apostles heard the call and followed Jesus, although not without difficulty and pain. One wonders what thoughts were on their minds as they stood by the cross and saw Jesus die. Did they wonder why they had been chosen, and what the call of God meant for them at that moment?

God has called each of us to be signs of love, to embody the gospel in our families, among our friends, where we work. When the call becomes difficult, when people refuse what we offer them, then perhaps we wonder, why me? There may be no answer, other than the free, loving will of God who invites us to share in his work. God's invitation, a sign of his trust, always carries with it the power to do what is asked. Our dignity lies in the fact that we are invited to share in the work of Jesus, and that we are called to be like him, looking at the success of our work not through our eyes, but through his.

I hear your call to follow you, Jesus, and I ask, "Why me?" I have sometimes asked this from a feeling of frustration, but now I want to ask it from a sense of wonderment and awe. Why have you chosen me to share in your work? Can it be that you chose me simply because you love me?

Silence

Silence is a great teacher. Creative insights in our personal relationships and in our work come more easily when the mind is silent and reflective. Silence teaches us how to avoid scattering our energies and how to focus them through the quiet centering of our minds. As silence teaches us, it also gives us a strength and a sense of confidence that we otherwise cannot fully experience.

Silence is a great healer. Constant activity unbalances us, causing a disturbance in the way we feel about ourselves and in the way we think about our world. Silence restores balance and gives us the ability to experience peace and harmony within ourselves, and to be a source of harmony for others.

If you do not take time to be silent, to look quietly at nature, or to listen to God's voice within you, you rob yourself of the wholeness that is meant to be yours.

I will take the time to experience you in silence,
Lord. Help me to be quiet in your presence, that
I may learn from you and deepen my experience
of wholeness.

Wrong Notes

A famous pianist once said that if he played all the notes right, nobody would notice, but if he played just one wrong note, well, then everybody would notice. That is human nature. A mistake seems to clamor for attention more than the dozens of things that go along smoothly.

Many people ruin their day by brooding over mistakes. They forget the many things they did that went well, and concentrate on the things that went wrong. They lose perspective about their own performance as well as the performance of others, and their pride keeps them from tolerating anything in themselves that is imperfect.

Once we learn from our mistakes, we might do ourselves a favor by putting them out of our minds and concentrating on what went well. That would be a gentle and realistic way to face ourselves, a way that would enable us to end our day with a feeling of peace and thankfulness.

My life has been full of mistakes, Lord, and to the extent that I am culpable, I ask your forgiveness. But much of my life has been colored by caring and by success in your eyes, and for this, I give you thanks. Free me from the kind of pride and self-pity that keeps me from forgiving myself when something goes wrong. Free me from the lack of compassion that can't tolerate mistakes in others.

APRIL 17

True Riches

When we die, there are only two things that we will be able to take with us: the love with which we have lived our lives, and the good that we have done. Everything else, we will have to leave behind. The more we believe this, the more our priorities change.

When we die, it would not be surprising if we were to hear Jesus say, "Thank you for all you did for me." He will not express his gratitude for the possessions we will have amassed, or for the power that we will have exercised over others, but he will thank us for becoming like him and for sharing in his work. To hear his words of approbation will be a part of our joy in the agelessness to come, a joy that will be made full when we understand that Jesus recognizes us as one of his own.

Lord, may I not waste time putting my priorities in things that do not last. Give me the wisdom to live according to your gospel and to see with your eyes.

A P R I L 18

Life Everlasting

"And eternal life means to know you, the only true God, and to know Jesus Christ, whom you sent."

— John 17:3

This world's final power is death, but Jesus has transcended every power in the world. He has overcome death, and through his resurrection, he has promised us a life of unending communion with him. Because God's love for us is what it is, he has given us the gift to live with him in unbroken life after death, for God wishes his bonding love for us to be forever. This is the promise of the gospel. Without this promise, the gospel has no ultimate meaning.

Whatever begins in this world, our lives, our friendships, our love, all of these are destined to last without end. Through the goodness of God, our friendships and love have a value that transcends the present moment. It is only this promise of Jesus that makes them fully beautiful and gives them a meaning that is eternal.

My friendships are treasures, Lord, because you have taken them all into your own resurrected life. You measure the duration of my life and the lives of all whom I love by the duration of your own. You give eternal life to all those who truly believe in you. Thank you, Lord Jesus, for the beauty of this unending gift.

A P R I L 19

Doing the Impossible

"What is impossible for man is possible for God."

— Luke 18:27

Left to ourselves, we would find the gospel an impossible invitation to accept, an inconceivable message to follow. Who among us could always love his or her enemies as Jesus commanded us to do? Who would be able to die to himself or herself and perseveringly carry the cross with Jesus? Who would be able to live the beatitudes as Jesus taught them, or to have the faith and hope that Jesus asks us to have?

More concretely, think of the personal crises in your own life that seemed impossible to bear or to resolve. By whose power were you able to get through them? The wise person realistically senses his or her own limits. The faith-filled person knows that, when it is a question of living the gospel message, his or her limits do not matter. They do not matter because what is impossible for human beings is quite possible for God. And it is by the power of God that we live and move and have our being.

I am sometimes afraid, Jesus, because the demands of life seem too difficult. You say your burden is light, but oftentimes I find it heavy. Help me to see that I make it that way. Teach me to lighten it by trusting in you, you who are able to do what I cannot.

A P R I L 20

Mirror Christians

Whoever listens to the word but does not put it into practice is like a man who looks in a mirror and sees himself as he is. He takes a good look at himself and then goes away and at once forgets what he looks like.

— James 1:23–24

"Mirror Christians" forget easily. Their lives no longer adequately reflect the word they have heard or read, and they easily forget who they are called to be. People quickly forget things that cease to be important to them. "Mirror Christians" are those who have lost their enthusiasm for the word because their interest in it has died.

Enthusiasm for the word is a gift of God, but the gift cannot bear fruit if there is no openness to receive it. When we identify the attitudes that have killed our openness to God's word, we can ask for the healing that enables us to receive the gift. Then his word again becomes a part of us and defines for us who we are.

There were times in my life when I was a "mirror Christian," Lord. Those were the times when your word could find no home in me, because my lack of interest closed me off from you. I regret that, Lord. May my love remain strong and centered on you, that I might always know the joy that your word brings.

APRIL 21

The Silence of God

Perhaps God is never silent. Perhaps there are simply times when we do not hear. In any case, we perceive what seems to be God's silence, and it disturbs us.

We experience the silence of God whenever we are out of tune with him. If we are on different wavelengths, the experience of his presence may never get through to us. God appears silent to the selfish and the unloving.

God may seem silent to us whenever we cease pondering the words of Jesus. God revealed himself completely through his Son. If we forget the revelation of Jesus, we miss hearing the speech of God.

Sometimes we experience the silence of God because of an inadequate way of praying. It may help us to say less and listen more. God may seem silent because we give him so little chance to speak.

Sometimes God is silent so that he can see if we love him enough to follow him in the darkness. This silence is a precious gift because it strengthens our love.

Jesus, I acknowledge that you are mystery, and that your silence is a part of the mystery of who you are. Teach me to change those parts of my life that keep me from being attentive to you and experiencing your peaceful presence. And if I find nothing in me that causes your silence, then may my longing for you strengthen my fidelity and love.

A P R I L 22

Happiness

Everybody desires happiness, but many try to settle for less than God wants them to have. Our greatest happiness comes when we do what God does, when we give to others the caring and love that

God gives to us. But there are times when we try to find happiness in doing the opposite. Our own experience tells us whether or not this works.

Jesus gave us the way to happiness when he gave us the gospel. The more we understand the gospel, the more we understand where our happiness is. Of course, there is a price. Happiness only becomes possible to the degree that we die to ourselves and put on the mind of Christ.

Jesus, you want my happiness even more than I want it myself. I have often pursued happiness in the wrong ways, and wound up with pain instead. May I live my life unselfishly as you lived yours, that I might know the kind of happiness that only you can give.

APRIL 23

Full Time

From the day we fully begin to believe in Jesus as our God, there is no time or activity in our lives that can be lived away from his presence. For those who accept Jesus fully, there is no such thing as a part-time discipleship. The love of Jesus lays claim to all of our outer actions, and to all of our innermost attitudes and thoughts.

Parents who love their children never calculate the least amount they can do in order to fulfill their role as parents. Love makes such calculations irrelevant. People who love their work never ask how little they can put into it and still get by. People who love Jesus never ask how little they can do and still be his followers.

Love is proven by its generosity and completeness. It is a full-time way of life.

*I follow you, Jesus, but I have a tendency to
cut corners. My love is far from perfect, and
yet you continue to love me perfectly. May my
love grow in constancy so that my friendship
with you can deepen.*

APRIL 24

Life-Givers

"You are like salt for all mankind."

— Matthew 5:13

"You are like light for the whole world."

— Matthew 5:14

Some people come into our lives and we experience
them as life-giving. They radiate a peaceful, loving
acceptance of their life and its circumstances. They
radiate a sense of caring for others. Their lives reveal the possibilities of what our own lives can be.

Others come into our lives and we experience
them as destructive. They bring no sense of love
and caring, no sense of joy. No light radiates from
them because, in their preoccupation with themselves, they allow nothing to shine out to others.

If we know something of the gospel, we know
something of what Jesus meant when he called us
to be as salt and light. Let us be thankful for those
people in our lives who have been salt and light for

us. They have been true gifts of God, because they have revealed something to us of who God is.

Jesus, my light, may I catch fire through your light within me. May I give it to others, for this light is the most precious gift that I have to give. Teach me what this means in my own particular circumstances, so that your gospel may live in me and bear fruit.

APRIL 25

Waiting

A great deal of precious time is consumed by waiting. People wait in traffic, in the check-out line, at the restaurant. They wait for raises, promotions, for better times. Sometimes they even wait for God, for God makes his presence known only in his own time and in his own way.

The patient man who knows how to wait can endure until Jesus comes. In fact, the reality of the patient man's endurance is proof that the Lord is already with him.

The patient man knows that while he waits, he is still loved. And so he is willing to wait and trust, for he believes that God is wise, and that God does nothing that is not finally for the sake of love. The God who permits darkness is acceptable to the patient man, for he believes in God's promise that the experience of light will finally be his. A patient man will not be disturbed by waiting, for he knows that he will never experience God's presence in this life as fully as he might wish. And so he finds what he can in the present, and waits calmly for what will eventually be.

Jesus, may I not tire of waiting for you. If you permit darkness in my life, you do that for a reason, but I believe that it is a reason of love. Increase my faith, and may my waiting sharpen my love for you.

APRIL 26

Home

When we think of home, we usually think of a comfortable place to be, an earthly dwelling place that we call our own. But in the total context of our lives, "home" in the gospel takes on a broader, transcendent meaning.

Jesus told his disciples that there were many rooms in his Father's house, and that he was going there to prepare a place for them (Jn 14:2–3). When their time came to go home, they would experience Jesus offering them the gift of a marvelously different kind of life. The Bible tells us something about that life. St. Paul said, "For we know that when this tent we live in — our body here on earth — is torn down, God will have a house in heaven for us to live in, a home he himself has made" (2 Cor 5:1). The book of Revelation adds: "I heard a loud voice speaking from the throne: 'Now God's home is with mankind! He will live with them, and they shall be his people. God himself will be with them, and he will be their God. He will wipe away all tears from their eyes. There will be no more death, no more grief or crying or pain. The old things have disappeared' " (Rv 21:3–4).

People often fear the prospect of moving on to their new home, for they fear the unfamiliar. Only perfect love can cast out fear. The promise of our heavenly home is given to us by Jesus as an act of love. It is a promise meant to increase our joy in the present moment, for it gives our present moment a hope of fulfillment. What is most valuable in the present will never be lost, but instead it will be preserved in a loving union joined eternally in God.

Jesus, may I not fear your promise of the heavenly home that you have already prepared for me. I want to accept it with gratitude and joy. Increase my understanding of your love that reveals itself in the promise of eternal union with you.

APRIL 27

Paradox

A poor Oriental farmer lost the only horse he had. When the villagers heard that the horse had run off, they sympathized with the farmer and said, "Bad luck." The farmer answered, "Who can say?" On the next day, the horse returned home with ten other horses. When the villagers heard this, they returned and said, "Good luck." The farmer replied, "Who can say?" Later that day, while training one of the new horses, the farmer's son fell off the horse and broke his leg. Again, the villagers sympathized and said, "Bad luck." The farmer replied, "Who can say?" On the following day, an invading army came into the village and took all the young men away as captives. The farmer's son was not taken because of his broken leg.

Sometimes we succeed in getting what we think will be good for us, and it turns out to be a disaster. And sometimes apparent disaster turns out to be good fortune. Who has not experienced this paradox in his or her life? The constant flow of positives and negatives in our lives teaches us to flow freely with them, and not to get stuck by taking either pole too seriously.

The times of light and darkness in my life constantly flow into one another, Jesus, as summer changes into winter and back again. I learn from you that in this life, it will never be otherwise. Give me the insight and strength to flow freely in the stream of paradox with a calm and peaceful mind.

A P R I L 28

Peace

"Peace is what I leave with you; it is my own peace that I give you."

— John 14:27

In giving you his peace, Jesus lets you know that his peace is possible, even in the midst of surface turmoil and suffering. Why does it work that way?

Peace is God's gift, but we are often the instruments through whom his peace flows. Peace comes to us at our deepest level whenever we try to remove hatred, dishonesty, and darkness in our relationships with one another, and replace them with love, truthfulness, and light.

The best thing about being a peacemaker is that we do not have to be successful at it in order to receive peace for ourselves. We still gain by offering peace to others even when they do not accept it, because the effort causes peace to grow within ourselves. Peace is always a gift that grows within the hearts of those who offer it. The peacemakers are the ones who have the deepest experience of the peace of Jesus, a peace that goes beyond the surface turmoils of life.

Jesus, may I be an instrument of your peace, even in those situations where offering peace is painful to me. Unless I die to myself by loving and forgiving others, I will be unable to know your peace. Strengthen me that I might be a peacemaker.

APRIL 29

Trust

"Would any of you who are fathers give your son a stone when he asks for bread? Or would you give him a snake when he asks for a fish? As bad as you are, you know how to give good things to your children. How much more, then, will your Father in heaven give good things to those who ask him!"

— Matthew 7:9–11

Many people do not experience God's gifts because they expect nothing from him. That makes it hard for them to recognize the gifts that God does give to them. Others pray for things that, in God's providence, are not likely to be granted, because they are out of tune with the mind of God. The mind of God will always be beyond our total understanding, but we can believe that what is ultimately necessary for us, what is really most important, will always be given. Without this kind of trust, we lack the ability to sustain a loving relationship with God and to be thankful for the gifts he gives.

Jesus, there are times in my life when I have been disappointed, when I have felt that you had let me down. I do not judge these feelings, Lord. I only ask for inner healing, for the ability to trust in the Father even as you trusted. I am incapable of this trust on my own. Please send me your Spirit, that I may think with your mind, and be at peace with my life. This gift I do expect from you, for without it, I cannot live in the spirit of your gospel.

APRIL 30

Flexibility

An intoxicated person can fall off a ladder and often land on the ground unharmed. If a sober individual were to have a similar fall, the results would probably be quite different. The intoxicated person is more flexible. His intoxicated state enables him to flow with the fall without tenseness, making it more likely that he will avoid the broken bones that his sober counterpart might incur.

Intoxication is much too high a price to pay for all this flexibility, of course. But what if people could cultivate a flexibility of spirit that would enable them to flow with the bumps and difficulties of life? Their lack of rigidity and fear would protect them from the sharp edges of much unnecessary suffering by opening the way to a more peaceful acceptance of life's difficulties. Flowing with the inevitable bumps of life, they would avoid the psychological bruises incurred by those who insist on resisting what is inevitable.

How many of our own sufferings do we make worse due to the fear and rigidity with which we face them?

Help me, Jesus, to face the inevitable hardships of my life with a greater sense of calmness and flexibility. May I learn to avoid the unnecessary suffering that comes from my rigid refusal to accept what can't be changed.

MAY

MAY 1

Relationships

Some kinds of relationships carry with them a sense of joy and peace. They are characterized by a mutual caring and selflessness that results in genuine love. Other kinds of relationships bring sorrow and disturbance. They are characterized by an egoism that results in the false love of self.

Relationships succeed or fail for a number of different reasons. When they fail, we can learn much by searching for the reasons. That can also be true for those relationships that succeed. They are the teachers of love.

Jesus, I thank you for the gift of my human relationships. May I never take them for granted or approach them unconsciously. May I learn from my successful relationships as well as from my failed ones.

MAY 2

Transformation

To be transformed is to grow into the persons whom we are created to be. But it is impossible to experience transformation unless we first come to know who we are at the present moment.

People who imagine that they are virtuous, when in reality they are not, cannot be transformed. Not knowing themselves, they are unaware of those areas of their lives that are in need of change. Those who truly know themselves are the ones most likely to become who they were created to be. They have the capacity for growth. Honesty is the beginning of transformation into the mind of Christ, the source in whom Christians finally discover who they are.

Jesus, I want to know myself as you know me, so that I might see more clearly what keeps me from you. May I have the personal insight that will open me to receive your transforming power. May my life be transformed into a deeper communion with you.

MAY 3

Ending the Day

Before you retire, take time to recall how God touched your life during this particular day. Perhaps he revealed himself in a friend's love, in something beautiful that you saw, or in a quiet experience of his own presence deep within you. In the rush of our activities, it is easy to forget the many touches of God's hand throughout the day. Recalling the touches of his presence reminds us of his love, sharpens our awareness of his gifts, and deepens our gratitude for his faithfulness. In being mindful of God's goodness, we understand how deeply we are loved.

Jesus, may I end this day aware of all the ways in which you have touched me with your love. As I remember how you have been with me this day, I thank you. I know that tomorrow will bring its own beautiful revelations of your presence. And so I want to end this day in gratitude, but also in a conscious anticipation of your presence that will renew itself when I awake.

M A Y 4

Too Good to Be True?

"Unless I see the scars of the nails in his hands and put my finger on those scars and my hand in his side, I will not believe."

— John 20:25

Is life ultimately benevolent? Does it cherish us, or are we finally betrayed by it? Perhaps that was Thomas' dilemma. It seemed too good to be true that Christ should have survived, that life should really be so good, that personal hope could still be kept alive. Perhaps Thomas is a paradigm for all of us. Haven't we had some doubts too?

Thomas, of course, was lucky. He was allowed to put his hands into the wounds and so he realized that Jesus' pains really were transformed into new life. And so Thomas could experience a renewed hope. But perhaps we should not envy him too much. Jesus said to Thomas, "Do you believe because you see me? How happy are those who believe without seeing me!" (Jn 20:29).

It was your resurrection, Jesus, that proved life will not betray us, that ultimately life is benevolent. I have not seen, but I want to believe. Your Spirit within me is the gift that enables me to believe. May I be a joyful witness to the fullness of life you promise, and to the hope that you give.

M A Y 5

Living Belief

Belief that is not dynamically lived will tend to languish and lose its power. One needs to ask, "Has my belief in Jesus made a difference in my life? Am I living with the power of his presence? If I had never heard of Jesus, would my life be pretty much the same as it is now?"

If our belief makes us joyful persons, people who gladly serve others, people who hope in life's goodness, then we are being enlivened by its power. Our belief not only invigorates us, but it spreads its life-giving qualities to the lives of those we touch. It is perhaps one of the most important gifts that we can share with another. And if our belief does not have this life-giving quality, are we willing to pray that Jesus' love and power might touch us and turn us into believers who radiate hope and joy?

Lord of all life, I pray for a belief that will enliven my life and bring hope to the lives of others. May my belief change the way I live and make me a bearer of joy to those whose lives I touch.

M A Y 6

A Worldly God

If you want to find God, look for him in the midst of your everyday life. He speaks to you in the ordinary events that touch you each day. If you find that too prosaic, too mundane, you may miss his voice and lose the opportunity to sense his presence.

We never know the means God will use to encounter us. World happenings, television programs, friendships, misunderstandings, good feelings, and sufferings — God uses all of these to say something about himself, about ourselves.

If our hearts are open, attentive, and silent, we will hear the message.

My perceptions have been dull, Jesus, and I have often missed your voice in the midst of my everyday life. Sharpen my faith that I might be more convinced of your eagerness to speak to me. Sharpen my consciousness that I might be more attentive to you.

119

Through Distorted Glasses

No two individuals see reality in quite the same way. Sometimes the lens through which we see distorts our vision. Those who see people through the lens of mistrust will not be comfortable with what they see. Those who view God through the lens of fear or ignorance will not discover the loving God. On the other hand, people who see life through the lens of love will discover a oneness with God, and with all creation that flows from God's love.

No one ever saw life more clearly and more truly than Jesus did. His vision was the vision of God, and he saw reality as it was — imperfect, but always loveable. The more our vision approaches that of Jesus, the more truly we see.

I know that my vision of reality is distorted, Jesus, but I don't always understand the seriousness of the distortion. May I see reality as you see it, so that I might see it and love it as it really is.

MAY 8

Tell the Good News

"Simon, son of John, do you love me more than these others do?" "Yes, Lord," he answered, "you know that I love you." Jesus said to him, "Take care of my lambs."

— John 21:15

You have to admire Peter and the apostles. The attitudes of the officials made it risky business for them to speak about Jesus. But Jesus meant so much to them personally, that they were unable to keep quiet about him. In our own times, we do not have the same threat the apostles experienced, but we have other subtle pressures that work to keep us quiet. How often do people feel free to talk about Jesus with their friends? Why are we so unwilling to share with others what God means to us? Without that kind of sharing, we miss something of God's presence.

Peter cared for Jesus' sheep at some risk to himself. If we decide to join him, we will discover some risk to ourselves too, because when we share something personal and important, we become vulnerable and open. But then, that is the whole point.

Jesus made himself vulnerable to Peter. "Do you love me, Peter?" What if Peter had said, "No"? "Will you feed my sheep, Peter?" What if Peter had said, "No"? That is always the risk. Jesus says to us, "Do you love me?" What if we say, "No"? Jesus asks, "Will you make my love known in the world?" And in asking that, he makes himself vulnerable.

May I not be afraid to speak about you, Jesus, or to reflect your values in my life. May I not be afraid of ridicule. Fill me with the courage to make your name known by the way I live your word and to be vulnerable as you were vulnerable.

Resting in His Hand

"My sheep listen to my voice; I know them, and they follow me. I give them eternal life, and they shall never die. No one can snatch them away from me."

— John 10:27–28

This is meant to be a gospel of consolation, and for those who love and trust God, it is. If we want to remain in God, nothing can take us away from him. The ultimate meaning of our lives will be realized — we will be one with life, and we will stop hurting ourselves by living apart from it. God gives that promise if we want it, and it is a promise of love, a promise that, ultimately, things will be right for us. We believe that we shall be one with God and experience the peace of that oneness. No one can snatch this away from us.

In the meantime, some of our temporal plans and concerns can take wrong turns. And yet, even here, we are in the hands of God. God works through our failures too if we allow him to do so.

Being in the hands of God does not mean an absence of pain or temporal failures. But it does mean that we will not be swallowed up by our pain and mistakes. Jesus himself seems to have made a mistake, from the human point of view. He chose Judas. But even that was turned into something good. From the pain of the cross came the resurrection. That is finally what it means to be in the hands of God. At the very end, we win.

Jesus, may I be content to remain in your hands when there is darkness in my life. If I know how to rest there, I will begin to understand that no one can snatch me away from you. In you is my peace.

M A Y 10

Letting Go of Preconceptions

It would be easier to love others if they would meet our expectations. We have preconceived ideas of what people should be like, and if they live up to those ideas, we love them. The same is often true about our love for God. As long as our preconceived ideas are met, we can find a certain kind of happiness. But eventually, we discover a big problem with that. People are hardly ever what we want them to be, and unless we see God as the saints do, God is never quite what we want him to be either. And so we are in danger of being disappointed in our relationships with God and with others.

To love sacrificially means to accept and love life as it is, and others as they are. That is the real miracle of life and it results in a new state of consciousness. As long as we struggle with this, we are not at peace. But we need to accept even our lack of peacefulness, if that is where we are. When we accept things as they are, we love ourselves and others unconditionally, the way God loves us. Perhaps that is the only kind of love that offers ourselves and others a power to change.

You do not ask me to love what people do, Jesus, but to love who they are. May I understand the distinction.

M A Y 11

Presence

"And I will be with you always, to the end of the age."

— Matthew 28:20

Because God loves what he has made, he is with us always. But his presence is noticeable and fruitful for us only if we become aware of it. There has to be a desire for this awareness; otherwise we fail to notice what is always all around us and within us. How can we become aware of God's presence in our lives? A lot depends on our willingness to see reality in a new way.

Whenever we serve one another with a self-giving love, we open ourselves to an awareness of God, because we become more like God. When we love, we experience the way God is toward us. Those who serve others in their families and communities are the ones most likely to have a holistic understanding of how God is present within them.

For other people, God is most deeply experienced in moments of quiet meditation. In their inner stillness, they come to know that God is truly within them. Jesus said his kingdom is within us. Those who experience this know the love of God, and they radiate his peace to those around them.

I want to believe that you are with me until the end of the world. May I discover this promise in my life by paying attention to where you are to be found.

M A Y 12

Seeing Beyond the Pain

God teaches us through our sufferings, especially the ones we cause to ourselves, and that probably counts for about ninety percent of all our sufferings. People who live for themselves probably suffer more disappointment in life than those who live for others. That is true especially for people who pass their time in self-pity and resentment. Resentments can be so strong and so deep-seated that they cause physical illness. Maybe God gives us a message through these kinds of symptoms.

Peace is the gift that flows from our willingness to listen to the message of God that comes through our sufferings. The Spirit of God reveals his presence in all situations of human life to those who are willing to listen. That is one of the reasons why the gospel tells us not to be afraid. Not that frightening things may not happen. But we have the power to overcome because of the Spirit of Jesus within us. In him is our hope and our peace, if we are willing to listen to the way he speaks to us.

Instead of rebelling against the unavoidable sufferings I cannot change, Lord, may I learn to hear what you are saying to me through them.

Oneness

"Love one another, just as I love you."
— John 15:12

The ideal of love and oneness can still exist in an imperfect world. Generous people continue to serve others even when they feel they are not appreciated. Sick wives and husbands persevere in trying to care for the needs of one another. Caring persons, in spite of their tiredness, still open their hearts to those who need their love.

Jesus offers all of us the power to become one with each other. The gospel is the good news because it saves us from meaningless isolation. Our willingness to serve others creates in us a sense of belonging to our brothers and sisters, and the price of experiencing this is self-forgetfulness. When self-forgetting love becomes a way of life, we begin to understand the gospel, and the joy of Jesus' command to be one.

I will never experience my oneness with others, Jesus, unless you give me the strength to pay less attention to myself and more attention to others. I know this from my own personal history. My ability to be one with others comes from the power of your presence within me. May I be responsive to this power.

The Honorable Bird

One of the symbols of the Holy Spirit is a dove, a symbol of the loving peace of God. Who is the Holy Spirit? Who would feel confident to wrestle with that question on his or her own? A Japanese inquirer once said to a priest, "I think I understand about the Father and the Son, but I can't figure out the meaning of the honorable bird." For many Christians too, the "honorable bird" is the great unknown.

The Bible tells us something about the Holy Spirit. The Holy Spirit is the fullness of what God has to give. The Holy Spirit strengthens and consoles us. The Holy Spirit melts our coldness. He helps us and offers us wholeness. He deepens our lives, and he brings light into our darkness. By means of his fire within us, he wants to renew the face of the earth.

If there is enough fire within us to offer hope and caring to our brothers and sisters, if sometimes we experience the peacefulness promised by Christ, then we know something of the Holy Spirit. The Holy Spirit is closer to us than we imagine, but unless we are deeply conscious of our lives, we may miss his presence.

Lord Jesus, fill me with the life of your Spirit. I ask that the fire of the Holy Spirit might enkindle a deeper life of conscious love within me, and that my desire for his presence might deepen and grow.

Peace Be to You

Jesus had been rejected by those he loved, and he had suffered a horrible death. Maybe his followers feared a similar fate. In any case, after the death of Jesus they were a frightened bunch, helplessly huddled behind locked doors in the same room where they had shared the last supper with Jesus.

In the midst of these frightened people, Jesus came to bring an experience of freedom and renewed life. He gave them his peace, and the gift of the Holy Spirit. We know what this gift means by its effects. It changed the disciples. Fearful people became courageous and filled with life. The doors of the room where they hid themselves burst open, and the disciples courageously shared the Good News.

What happened to the disciples in the upper room can happen to us. That is one of the great meanings of Pentecost, the coming of the Spirit. But we already have that Spirit. We just do not always recognize it. Once you believe that this power is within you, you can be free. The disciples had to be freed from fear, and perhaps from a certain lack of faith and trust. What is it that you need to be freed from? What anxieties, fears, resentments, or cynicisms keep you from the peace and joy Jesus gives? Will you let go of these things and allow the power of the Spirit to heal you?

Your Spirit brings fullness of life, Lord. Fill me with this Spirit that I might become the person you created me to be.

Tenderness

Mothers should be remembered all year long, but their special day of remembrance occurs in May. Mothers reflect the tenderness of God, and they are the gifts through whom we receive the gift of life. Reflecting on the gift, we can only respond with gratitude, for we have known tenderness.

In Isaiah 49:15, God asks if a mother can forget her infant, or be without tenderness for the child of her womb. And God says that even if she does forget, he will never forget us. On the palms of his hands, he has written each of our names.

God regards all of us with empathy and kindness, but many people are unaware that this is the way God is. If we are aware of God's gift of tenderness in our own lives, perhaps we can pass it on to others. People may find it hard to believe that God is kind if they do not experience kindness from one another.

Thank you, Lord, for all mothers everywhere, but especially I thank you for my own. I thank you too for the gift of your own tenderness. May I give to others what I have received.

Life to the Full

"I have come in order that you might have life — life in all its fullness."

— John 10:10

What does "life in all its fullness" really mean for us in this present moment? Part of the meaning would seem to be in loving life as it is. There is really no other way to love it. Either you love it as it is, accepting what cannot be changed, or you do not love it fully at all. The same would be true in our love for others. Their actions may not always be loveable, but we would continue to love them in their essential personhood as they are. Perhaps this kind of love requires a miracle, because it means not allowing our feelings to get in the way of what is ultimately real. We often find that difficult.

Fullness of life in this world comes when we love even when we realize those we love will never be perfect, that they will never be fully who we would like them to be. But we pour out our love toward them anyway. To do otherwise would mean that our love would remain stuck within ourselves. That would not be the fullness of life. Rather, it would be the beginning of psychological and spiritual putrefaction. Without the power of God in our lives, this would eventually be our fate.

Jesus, you offer us fullness of life, a way of life that brings wholeness and peace. And yet, there is much within me that keeps me from completely accepting your gift of fullness of life. I ask your pardon for my blindness and obstinacy. Show me where I need healing, and strengthen me with your loving presence.

Forgetting

A woman had been deeply hurt by her husband. Finally, after a long period of time, she smiled weakly at him and said, "I forgive you." And then her face froze as she said, "But I'll never forget."

There is a sense in which we cannot help remembering the hurts of life. Sometimes they pop back into our minds without our consent. But when the remembrance is intentional, when we do not want to let go of remembering, then perhaps there is no real forgiveness. In any case, few of us would be content with the kind of unforgetting forgiveness given by the woman in the story.

Forgiveness is one of the heroic acts of life. Love makes real forgiveness possible. Such forgiveness is a gift of God who constantly extends it to us. It is a forgetting forgiveness, the only kind that results in full reconciliation and peace.

Jesus, may the quality of my forgiveness be of the same quality as yours. May I forgive as I would wish to be forgiven.

Foolishness

It is foolish to enjoy doing wrong. Intelligent people take pleasure in wisdom.

— Proverbs 10:23

Foolishness, in the Old Testament, was usually equated with sinfulness. It referred to people who chose to walk in the ways of selfishness instead of in the ways of the Lord. Foolish people caused harm to others, and they did not escape from harm themselves, for the path of selfishness is always a tragic path.

Does our own experience bear this out? Few people can say that they never intentionally acted foolishly. Sometime in our own lives we too have probably given in to foolishness in the Old Testament sense. One can imagine how therapeutic it might be to evaluate the results of our own foolishness. The evaluation would be essential for the avoidance of what is morally unhealthy in our own lives. Wouldn't it be true that those who fail to evaluate the tragedy of their foolish actions are condemned to repeat them?

Holy Spirit, fill me with the wisdom to know when my own paths are not straight, and give me the courage to walk in your ways.

M A Y 20

Marks of Love

You would think that Jesus would have wanted to forget the wounds of his passion, but after his resurrection, he insisted on showing them to his apostles. The wounds were more than signs of his identity. They were signs of his love. For those disciples who knew how to look at them with understanding, the wounds revealed a God whose love would stop at nothing. This was the message that Jesus came to share with us.

Once you see the wounds of Jesus, you know how deeply and irrevocably God is committed to you. What is there that God would not do for you? What ultimate good would he not give you? What darkness would he not dispel with his light?

Your love for me did not end with your earthly life, Jesus. It continues into eternity. You said so in so many different ways. Increase my faith in the presence of your love that touches me now, in this present moment.

M A Y 21

Labor Pains

When we are exhausted in our service to others, or when our caring is misunderstood, then we acquire our own personal wounds which are marks of love. No one can love without becoming wounded in some way, but the wounds are proclamations of a caring life. The pains and discomforts of our daily labor borne with love carry a positive message of a life spent in service for others.

We become physically tired as Jesus did. We are sometimes rejected as Jesus was. What happened to Jesus happens to us. As his wounds were marks of his love, so it is with ours. We can bear our labor pains with love, for nothing of lasting value is ever accomplished without them.

I have always looked negatively at my own fatigue and rejections, Lord. Let me see that there is another way to look at them. May I see them as signs of a love and fidelity that you make possible within me, and as a sharing in your life. Seeing them in this way, may I come to accept these labor pains with gratitude.

M A Y 22

Do Not Lose Faith

"Do not be worried and upset," Jesus told them. "Believe in God and believe also in me."

— John 14:1

Jesus said these words on the night before he was crucified. This was a night full of sadness for the disciples, and so Jesus was requesting a lot when he asked them to have faith.

It was on this night before the crucifixion that the disciples listened with shock as Jesus predicted his betrayal. Then Jesus told his disciples that he was going away and that he would no longer be visibly present to them. And later, when Peter professed his loyalty, Jesus told Peter that he too would deny him. But through all of this sorrow and tragedy, Jesus told his disciples that he would not leave them alone.

Jesus never promised that our lives would be without conflicts, but he did promise to be with us through them. And in the end, he promised that we would be victorious over them. Our challenge is to believe this, and it is Jesus' presence with us that makes this possible. Are we willing to persevere in our trust?

There is something in me that is afraid to trust, Lord, and yet my only chance of experiencing peace is to trust you. You understand my difficulty, Lord. Be patient with me and give me the courage that comes from your presence.

M A Y 23

Standards

I urge you, then — I who am a prisoner because I serve the Lord: live a life that measures up to the standard God set when he called you.

— Ephesians 4:1

Paul is talking about our call to know God and to respond to his love. But we cannot experience the call unless we are lovingly conscious of the life we have in this present moment. Where else is God to be found but in the present moment? If we are unconscious of that, we cannot see what it can reveal to us, and we miss God's presence within it. The most basic call we have from God is to be lovingly conscious of our life as it is given to us in the here and now.

Now this may seem like an obvious standard. Aren't most people naturally conscious of their lives? But how many of us really are? Are we always fully involved in each moment we live? And if the answer is "no," then how can we discern God's call in the midst of our unconsciousness?

Help me to stay awake, Lord, that I might not live my life as if I were half-asleep. I'll never hear you unless I'm attentive and alert to your presence as you come to me in each moment of my life.

M A Y 24

Reflections

We come to know the goodness of God when we see his goodness reflected in others. When we look at our husbands, wives, parents, children, friends and see them doing something loving, then we see something of God. Of course, we may have to catch them in a good mood first. But in people's better moments, when they are most truly themselves, we can look at them and see a reflection of God.

Only those who are truly conscious are able to see the reflections of God's goodness in others. For those who live in a fog, the reflections shine in vain. What a tragedy to miss the reflections of God. What a tragedy if we reflect nothing to others.

Your goodness emanates from so many people who cross the path of my life, but many times, Lord, I never noticed. For those times, and for all the occasions when my own life reflected little of you, I am sorry. Keep me alive to the reality of your goodness.

Disenchantment

Disenchantment comes when we realize that God does not act as we think he should. Enlightenment comes when we realize we ought to be happy about that.

God will often disappoint us if our preconceived notions fall short of reflecting who he really is. If we want to know what God is like, we have to reflect on Jesus. In doing that, we find an invitation to let go of our childish notions of God, much in the same way that we had to let go of the childish notions of our parents. But old notions die hard. What childish notions about God do we still keep deep within us? What kind of pain do these childish notions cause in our lives?

Lord, I've often wished for a God who would spare me suffering, but you died on the cross. I've often wished for a God who would let me off the hook, but you constantly accepted the challenges of life. I've often wished for a God who would get even with sinners, but you showed them mercy. No wonder I've had difficulty in accepting you as you are.

Which Foot Does the Job?

It takes two feet to walk, but which one, at any given moment, is the more important? Watch yourself when you walk. One foot does the work of supporting your weight, while the other hovers uselessly in the air. Or so it seems. Would it be possible, though, to get along without that apparently useless foot? If both feet are equally supporting you, you can stand but not walk. If both feet are in the air at the same time, you may be in trouble.

A successful life journey is made up of activity and restful prayer. In a healthy life, there is time for prayer, and time for activity. Life could not flow smoothly if one of these components were missing. Without prayer, we fall out of touch with God, as well as with ourselves. Without activity, God cannot fully express himself within us. There can be no fruitful activity without prayer, and no fruitful prayer without some kind of activity. Does your life include a balance of both?

My life is often out of balance, Lord, because I'm not convinced of the value of prayer. But without an awareness of your power in my life, my activities never bear the fruit that you intend. And how will I discover this unless I rest quietly with you in prayer, that I may know the guidance of your Spirit?

M A Y 27

The Common Bond

Jesus frequently told us to love our enemies. But why did he insist so much on this? What was the vision that lay behind his consistent command to love?

"Whoever loves me will obey my teaching. My Father will love him, and my Father and I will come to him and live with him" (Jn 14:23).

The life of God is within each of us, which means that all of us have our lives in God. This is the bond, stronger than blood, that makes us one. To hate another person is to hate the bond, and the bond is God. Not to love becomes the most tragic choice that we can make. If there has been hatred in us, our only excuse can be ignorance of the full significance of what we have done.

Lord, I don't fully understand the meaning of our common bond, our oneness in you. It seems too abstract. But at least let me believe it in faith, so that one day it might become more a part of my experience. Let there no longer be enemies in my life.

M A Y 28

Just for the Love of It

We tend to think that Jesus' life was successful because it was lived in caring service for others. And of course that is true. But Jesus also spent much time in solitary retreat and prayer. Jesus' disciples followed his example. Why all this emphasis on prayer?

We receive guidance and peace in the quietness of prayer, of course. There is, however, another reason for prayer, a more important reason, but one which may seem to be less practical. One prays simply because one loves. We spend time with a special friend not because we want something, but simply because we care for our friend. The more we experience this kind of friendship, the more our love for our friend grows. It has no immediate practical purpose. And yet, we cannot be fully human, or fully respond to those we love without this experience. It is the same in our relationship with God. We spend time with God because we love. It is from this experience that we grow in our ability to do what God asks of us, for our service is born from our love.

When I fully understand the meaning of loving you, Lord, I will no longer have to struggle so hard to find time for quietly loving you. Enlighten my understanding.

M A Y 29

Responding

One of my closest friendships began in a very strange way. One day after Mass, a lady came up to me and shoved a large paper sack into my hands. "Merry Christmas!" she said. "Enjoy." A week later, I sought her out to thank her, and she responded by inviting me to her home. Over the next two years our friendship grew as we shared our spiritual journeys and our common love for music. Although she died of cancer, the friendship continues, for our own lives continue.

This friendship began with an invitation. All friendships do. Can you recall this process in your own life?

Something similar happens in God's relationship with us. God calls us to friendship with himself. The invitation may come through prayer, through our conversation with someone, through reading, or even when walking under the stars. You never know when it will come, and so you always have to be awake to its possibility. The invitation comes often, but it may be that it is not often heard.

Perhaps I've grown deaf to your invitations, Lord. Because you are who you are, your invitation to friendship is constant in my life. May I understand and respond.

M A Y 30

Leave Your Homeland

When God called Abraham to be the father of a new nation, he told him to leave his homeland for another place that would be shown to him. Every call from God is an invitation to leave something so that we might be free for something else. What we are asked to "leave" is usually an attitude which restricts our possibilities for greater life. We are invited to free ourselves up, to grow, to be open to a broader vision of life, a broader vision of love.

When Jesus calls us to friendship, he asks us to leave the obstacles to the call, whatever they might be. At this present moment in your life, what are the obstacles that Jesus asks you to leave behind?

I have heard your call to friendship, Lord, but I haven't always been quick to answer you. My selfishness stands in the way, and it has compromised my freedom. I have preferred my old ways to the newness of your Spirit, and so I have missed the fullness of your friendship. But it is not too late, Lord, for your invitation to friendship is constant. Thank you. May I love enough to respond to the many ways in which you invite me.

M A Y 31

An Inside Job

A well-known painting portrays Jesus standing before a door, knocking to gain entrance. When someone pointed out to the artist that the lack of an outer door handle would prevent Jesus from entering, the artist replied, "There's no knob because the door represents the human soul. It can only be opened from the inside."

How could it be otherwise? There is no force in love, only free acceptance. And so God waits for us. Perhaps nothing so beautifully illustrates the love and humility of God than his patient waiting.

Learning from the humility of God, perhaps we might be humble enough to wait for the responses of one other. Responses can only come from the inside in the fullness of their own time. No one knows exactly when that is. In the meantime, a love that is deep and humble is willing to wait patiently with hope.

Lord, thank you for your patience with me. May I imitate your patience as I wait for the responses of others.

JUNE

Everything in Its Own Time

A boy wanted to pick a peony to give to his mother for her birthday. But when he went to pick one from the garden, he discovered that all of the peonies were still in the budding stage. With a look of disgust, he picked the largest bud and tried to force it open. But when he finished, he had completely ruined the budding flower. What would have become a beautiful large red peony was simply a mashed mass of half-formed petals in his hand.

All things bloom in their own time. That is especially true for human beings. Unfortunately, we never know how long that is going to take. And so it makes sense to be patient with the efforts of others as well as with our own. Otherwise, we risk the danger of forcing what should not be forced, and of expecting more than can be given.

God shows his gentleness by expecting no more of us than we are able to give. We need to show that same kind of gentleness to others and to ourselves.

Lord, give me patience with myself and with others, the same kind of patience that you have with me. May I learn to accept limitations, and not to cause harm through unreasonable expectations.

J U N E 2

Selfless Love

Religion is not simply a matter of dogma and ritual but rather a matter of becoming more conscious of God as a friend, someone you love simply because of who he is. Religion is meant to be an experience of the God who loves us, and an experience in which all people become friends because they are bonded together by a common belief in God's love.

Loving God fully, we would love God not for what we get from him, nor for the joy he gives us, but simply because God is who he is. And we would love others in the same way, simply because they are who they are. This is the way God loves, and being made in his image, we are called to reflect the kind of selfless love that God continually shows to all of us.

If I learn to love selflessly, Jesus, I will come to know something of the love you have for me. That gift can come only from you. May my heart be open to receive it.

Letting Go

In the story of Mary and Martha (Lk 10:38–42), Martha complained that Mary did nothing more than sit at the feet of Jesus, while she herself was left with all the work. Jesus responded to the complaint by saying that Mary had chosen the better part and that it would not be taken from her, but he never did tell Martha to stop working. He did tell her though that she was anxious about many things. Perhaps her anxiety might have caused her to be less conscious of his presence, or perhaps the anxiety made it difficult for her to experience her work as a joy. Her worries might have kept her from the delight of putting herself fully into what the present moment offered to her. And Jesus wanted to spare her from that. He also wants to spare us, and so he tells us not to be anxious as we do in life what we have to do.

If there were no people depending on me, I might be able to work without anxiety, Lord. And yet, what good does my anxiety do? You ask me simply to do my best and to trust that I will have the strength to handle things, no matter how they turn out. I will do my best, and then let go.

Cradled in God's Love

"Can a woman forget her own baby,
and not love the child she bore?
Even if a mother should forget her child,
I will never forget you.
Jerusalem, I can never forget you!
I have written your name on the palms
of my hands."

— Isaiah 49:15–16

These words were addressed to Jerusalem, a community treasured by God. We may also apply these words to ourselves as individuals, for that is the way God treasures each of us. In the midst of a day when many things go wrong, or in the midst of a day full of misunderstandings, we can rely on this love. Our only problem is that we forget, or that we do not fully believe that this kind of love can really be.

We experience the tenderness of God's love to the extent that we become aware of it and trust in it. God's promise is always with us. It has only to be accepted.

Lord, this seems too good to be true. Deepen my consciousness of your promise and help me to trust in it so that I might experience your peace in this moment.

Climbing the Mountain

A small community lived in a valley surrounded by mountains. For centuries, no one had ever left the valley. One day a young man decided to climb the mountains to see what lay beyond. The village elders discouraged him, saying that there was nothing beyond the valley. There never had been, and there never would be. It was always so.

But the young man decided to see for himself. He climbed the mountains and discovered different civilizations which had learned to write, make music, and create beautiful forms of art. When he came back with new visions for his own community, the elders ridiculed him. "You bring back lies," they told him. "There is nothing beyond this valley. There never has been. There never will be. It was always so."

What about our own life experience? Are we more like the young man, or more like the elders? What part of our thinking is still stuck in the valley? Are we willing to expand our vision and broaden our minds beyond our ordinary everyday experiences? What would that mean for us?

I don't always find comfort in taking risks and learning new ways, Lord. Yet, you lead me beyond my valley, over the mountains, and into experiences that bring more consciousness, more life. I don't want to be afraid of growth. May I hunger for it.

Revelation

"I have told you this while I am still with you. The Helper, the Holy Spirit, whom the Father will send in my name, will teach you everything and make you remember all that I have told you."

— John 14:25–26

In one sense, revelation was completed with the coming of Jesus Christ. In another sense, revelation continues as the Holy Spirit instructs us through our own life experiences, through the events of our own times. The message of love remains the same, but the Holy Spirit helps us to apply it in our present-moment situations. Truly, God does not leave us orphans. His creative Spirit is with us. Our task is to become conscious of this presence and what it says to us, listening silently for the inspiration of the Holy Spirit, and selflessly following where it leads us. Through our silent listening, and through listening to others who are imbued by the Spirit, we will be able to discern the movement of God as he works in our present moment.

I want to understand what you are saying to me now, Holy Spirit, through the present events of my life and through the truth of my own personality. May I come to understand your revelation more deeply, and follow it with greater fidelity and love. Teach me how to read the signs of your presence.

Thankfulness for the Past

Without our own unique past experiences, we would not be the persons we are. The love we have received, the knowledge we have gained are all gifts from people who have influenced our lives. Some of these people we have known personally. Others lived long before we were born, and their ideas have influenced us from the distant past. To all of these individuals, we owe our thanks. Most of us, for example, have received our faith from our parents, and yet we all owe a debt of gratitude to the original apostles of Jesus Christ. If they had not preached about Jesus, how would we have known about him?

Part of the joy of life is in the realization of how much we have received from others, especially from those who have been closely bonded to us. This realization increases love, and the love deepens the bonds. And through our gratitude, we come to understand more clearly who we are.

I ask, Lord, for the awareness to appreciate what I have received. What I have become is due largely to the wisdom and love which others have shared with me as a gift. May my gratitude deepen.

The Most Important Gifts

What do you want most from God? What do you think God would most want to give to you? Perhaps the deepest desire of God would be to give you the gift of being conscious of him in your daily life, along with the power to understand his love and to share the gift of that love with others. If you look at the words of Jesus in scripture, these seem to be the gifts God is most desirous of giving to all of us. Are these the gifts that you would most want to receive from God?

I admit, Lord, that my desires are not always for those things that are the most important in life. I want to understand what the most important gifts of life are, so that I might desire to receive them from you. Expand the scope of my vision.

Awareness

A sister was dying, and she wondered if she would get to heaven. A friend reminded her of her years of faithful service, the many kindnesses she had rendered to others, all the things she had done for God. The list of good deeds surprised her, for she never felt she had done very much for anybody.

The sister's attitude was humble, but also maybe a little dangerous. When people do not clearly see how God's love and power have worked in them, how can they give adequate thanks for their lives?

I want to be more aware of the value of my life for others, Lord, because I want to give you thanks for what you have accomplished in me. Your power within me was your gift to me. The acceptance of that power was my gift to you. As I look back over my life, I give you thanks for what you and I together have made of it for your glory, and for the good of others.

JUNE 10

Trinity

What did God have in mind in revealing God's identity as the Trinity: Father, Son, and Holy Spirit? Perhaps we can find meaning in this revelation if we look at our own lives.

Can any of us truly exist without being in relationship with others? We never could have passed through our infancy without relationships with those who nurtured us. We could not have passed successfully through childhood and adolescence without relationships with others which revealed to us who we were. And what kind of meaningful adult experiences would we have had without relationships that enabled us to love and to learn that we are loved? Human beings exist and grow through their myriad communications with others.

God reveals to us that we were made in his own image. Would this mean that God exists in relationships too? Would this mean that within the very essence of God there is a continual dynamic flow of love and communication? How this can be is a mystery to us, but God has revealed that his life consists not in loneliness, but in relationship. And since we are made in God's image, this revelation tells us something quite clear about ourselves.

Lord, I need freedom from the selfish isolation with which I live much of my life. It is a denial of what I am meant to be. May I have the courage to trust in a life of relationships and to live in your image.

J U N E 11

Prayer

Some people find the idea of prayer to be quite boring. But would that change if people understood prayer as a loving consciousness of God in the events of their everyday lives? Perhaps then the love shown to them by their friends would speak to them of the source of love. And if they gave thanks to God, that would be prayer. Seeing a sky lit up by thousands of points of starlight would remind them of the source of its beauty. And if they gave thanks to God, that would be prayer. Seeing their own gifts would remind them to be grateful to the source of all gifts. And if they gave thanks to God, that would be prayer. Would this kind of prayer be a source of joy in their lives?

If I understood prayer in this way, Lord, would I become more fully alive?

JUNE 12

Dying

Some people die with fear, or with bitterness toward life, while others die with hope and gratitude for what they have received. The attitudes with which we die are formed throughout our lives. We create them by the way we respond to the individual tests of life as they confront us each day.

Every choice we make has a threefold consequence. Each choice affects our present moment, our moment of death, and the way we will experience the timeless freedom of everlasting life. Each moment of our lives is precious not only for the present, but also for the future. Making the wrong choices stifles the growth that God offers us through his gift of life. We give meaning to the gift through the choices that forge our personalities in this life and in the life beyond.

How I will die, Lord, is known to you alone. Help me to live this present moment well. If I can persevere in doing that throughout my life, I will have no worries about the future.

JUNE 13

Answers

"And so I say to you: Ask, and you will receive; seek, and you will find; knock, and the door will be opened to you."

— Luke 11:9

The promise of Jesus is that our prayers will be answered. Is that too good to be true? Perhaps that all depends on how you understand the promise. If you were completely in tune with the mind of God, then your prayers would be answered in the way that you wished. The more the thoughts of God become your own, the more the promise of Jesus becomes positively fulfilled in your life. If you come to know something of the mind of God through prayer and reflection on scripture, you will know what to ask for in prayer. And because what you ask will be in accord with the mind of God, it will be granted to you.

Sometimes you meet people who tell you that their prayers are always answered. Do you suppose they have discovered the secret of how the promise is fulfilled?

I know, Lord, that my prayers are always answered, even when my requests have to be denied. But I would like to be more in tune with the movement of your Spirit, so that my prayers might be in accordance with your will.

J U N E 14

Loosening Up

Have you ever noticed that the harder you try to get rid of a fault, the more it seems to stay with you? There might be a simple solution to the problem. Just loosen up and don't try so hard. That may seem like a bogus solution, but consider how it works in other areas of your life.

Have you ever tried so hard to improve your game of golf or tennis that you tied your body in knots with the effort? Your performance probably got worse until you learned to loosen up. The same thing holds true when you strive too much for success in your personal relationships, or when you strain to master material that you are trying to learn. Maybe sometimes you stand in your own way by trying too hard.

Loosening up does not mean caring less about what you are doing. It simply means using your energy without anxiety so that you become more efficient at what you want to do.

It seems paradoxical, Lord, that I might be more efficient in doing your will if I stopped trying so hard to do it. Perhaps if I lived less tensely I could avoid stumbling over myself and spoiling my own efforts.

JUNE 15

A Sword

"Do not think that I have come to bring peace to the world. No, I did not come to bring peace, but a sword."

— Matthew 10:34

Strange words from the one whom we call "Prince of Peace!" And are these words not out of character for the one who so often promised us peace? But it is true that Jesus' words may well seem like a sword because of the divisions within ourselves. We

155

are sometimes so out of step with his message that his words cut through our lives like a sword. If the pain deepens the realization that we are out of step with Jesus, the sword will be the beginning of our healing. Allowing his power to heal our inner divisiveness prepares us for the experience of peace. His words no longer cut through our lives like a sword when we learn how to accommodate our lives to them. But for someone who is not fully pliant, the way to peace is experienced as a sword that cuts through the stiffness of an unreceptive heart.

My own lack of openness to you turns your presence into a sword. Is it true, Lord, that the experience of the sword in my life can actually be a prelude to peace? Help me to understand and accept your word that I might experience it not as pain, but as peace.

JUNE 16

The Cross

What if Christ had never died on the cross, but instead, had exercised his power and come down before his death, resplendent in his victory over those who crucified him? Would this have been a better ending of his ministry to us, or would it have been worse? But if Jesus had not endured the fullness of the cross, how would we have known the depth of his love? If Jesus had come down from the cross, how could we have believed in God's ability to be compassionate in the face of our own suffering?

If we escaped our sufferings by coming down from our own crosses, would our ability to love be compromised? Would we be able to experience compassion for others in their sufferings?

Teach me to learn something from my own sufferings, Jesus. May they not lead me to self-pity or despair, but to a selfless kind of love and to compassion for others in their sufferings.

JUNE 17

The God Who Knows

He always had the nature of God, but he did not think that by force he should try to become equal with God. Instead of this, of his own free will he gave up all he had, and took the nature of a servant. He became like man and appeared in human likeness.

— Philippians 2:6–7

God is one who shows solidarity with our weakness. He understands it because he experienced it, and this is one of the most beautiful attributes of God. In your depressed moments, you can never say to God, "You don't know what it's like." In Jesus, God has experienced human thirst, rejection, betrayal, and even a death that seemed hopeless. Are you misunderstood and sometimes even abandoned by those you love? God knows. The "fullness of all being" suffered these things too. And because of this, you can believe more deeply that his compassionate presence is with you in your own sufferings.

Thank you, God, for sharing in my life. Through your incarnation, you have enabled me to believe that you understand me. You have made it easier for me to trust you.

JUNE 18

Dying Before Our Time

In Mt 25:14–30, Jesus tells the story of a ruler who gives three of his servants a certain number of silver pieces. Two of the servants use their silver pieces wisely, so that they wind up with more than they had. Their master praises them for their resourcefulness. The third man, out of fear of his master, simply buries his silver piece so that he will not lose it. However, by burying the silver piece, he incurs his master's wrath.

St. Iranaeus said that the glory of God is a person who is fully alive. How many of us die before our time by not using our gift of life to the fullest? Is there some part of your life that remains buried and unlived because of your fear?

I have at times yielded to apathy and fear of failure, Lord, and so the full gift of life you have given me has lain unused. I had begun to die before my time, but through the presence of your love, may I continue to revive while the opportunity still exists.

JUNE 19

Responsibilities

"And you are my friends if you do what I command you."

— John 15:14

Is it possible to have a mutual friendship without responsibilities? On God's part, there is his promise that he will be faithful and lovingly present to us. That is God's responsibility to us. On our part, there must be a positive response to the love offered. That would be our responsibility to God. Of course, our response to God does not buy his love. We have that anyway. But without a positive response, we never come to experience what God's love is. It shines on us, but our unresponsiveness keeps us from seeing it.

Our responsibilities to God are not meant to be burdens, but opportunities for us to experience who God is by becoming more like him. How else can we know him and be his friends? When God asks us to be a responsible partner in the friendship, he does so in order that we might understand who we are meant to be.

You and I have looked at this question of responsibility from different points of view, Lord. For me, responsibility sometimes seems like a burden. You see it as an invitation to love. May I come to see responsibility as a freedom to be enjoyed and not as a burden to be endured.

Crossing the Chasm

A deep chasm often separates us from others. Our prejudices and locked-in opinions create the chasm that divides us from people whose ideas are different from our own. And so we miss the opportunity to learn from their experiences. We miss a possible opportunity for growth and for the enrichment of our own experiences.

What might happen if we decided to jump across the chasm to see what could be learned from the ideas and experiences of others? If there were something to be learned, we would return enriched with a broader vision of truth. And if there were nothing to learn, we would come away strengthened in our own truth.

Chasms are dangerous because sometimes they leave us with an incomplete understanding of things. Then they become obstacles to a fuller vision of life.

Jesus, may I discover the freedom of an open mind. I never want to choke off the possibility of learning new things, of discovering something that will broaden my horizons of truth and my appreciation for others.

On Fire

The apostles shared the Good News of Jesus because they became so conscious of God's goodness that they could hardly do otherwise. They were so on fire with their experience of God's love that they were unable to keep it to themselves. Perhaps people should pray for the kind of fire that the apostles seemed to have had. Much is lost in life when the awareness of God's goodness remains unshared.

The Good News is God's gift, but we can predispose ourselves and others to it by what we say and do. If people become more conscious of God's presence in their lives because of us, then the fire is catching, and our lives become a great gift to others. When we allow God's love to change us, we are able to do what the apostles did. We bring God to a world that needs so much to be healed through his love.

Lord, may those of us who follow you catch fire from one another. Let my life be so full of spiritual energy that I will be unable not to spread the fire of your love.

JUNE 22

Ecology

God looked at everything he had made, and he was very pleased.

— Genesis 1:31

God made the heavens and the earth, and he was pleased because they reflected his goodness. Since everything that God creates reflects something of himself, it seems an insult to God when we spoil and ruin the reflection. Is there something in our own lifestyle that adds to the spoiling of God's reflection in the things he has made? Do we misuse the goodness of the earth and endanger the lives of those who will come after us? The question can be addressed to the human community as a whole, or to people as individuals. It is on the individual level that immediate changes can be made. How can we as individuals eliminate the wasting of precious resources and the polluting of the environment in which we live?

I haven't given much thought to the ways in which I abuse the gifts of this world, Lord. The gifts of nature are really your gifts, and I haven't thought much about that either. I have probably wasted just about everything, Lord, from the heat, water, and electricity in my home to the food that I take in cafeterias and leave on my plate. I am sorry for my own part in wasting your gifts and also for the times I have trashed my environment by not keeping it clean.

J U N E 23

Expectations

Is it true that our expectations affect our happiness in life? If we rise in the morning with the expectation that the day will yield nothing beautiful, our expectations will probably be fulfilled. The small joys that are a part of most of our days will pass by without our having recognized them.

Positive mindsets orient us to the possibility of positive experiences in our lives, so that we become more conscious of our ability to notice them, and even to create them. Negative mindsets accomplish the same results, but in reverse. Our expectations usually carry their own fulfillment in their wake. They are powerful factors in determining what our lives will be like.

Many of our expectations about life have become unconscious through long force of habit, but with a little conscious reflection, we can often bring them up to the surface of our minds where they can be examined. If we like what we find, then we can give thanks. If we are unhappy with our findings, our increased consciousness will give us the power to change.

Ultimately, you want me to find joy in my life, Lord. I believe that. May my expectations open my mind to become more conscious of the joys that I often miss.

JUNE 24

On Being Human

People sometimes feel guilty when they experience the very human emotions of anger, of impatience, or of fear which they sometimes equate with a lack of trust in God. But there is nothing wrong with the experiencing of those feelings. In fact, our lives would not be normal if we never felt their presence. Our uncomfortable feelings only become harmful when we consciously nurture them, or when we allow them to grow into actions that hurt either ourselves or others.

For peace of mind, we have to accept the uncomfortable side of our personalities, the emotions that we would rather avoid or eliminate from our lives. These emotions are simply a part of who we are, a part of what it means to be human. To feel guilty about them is to invest an energy in them that robs us of the strength we need for more important things.

God treasures us in our humanness. We should treasure ourselves as God does, as the fully-human people that he made us to be, including the sides of us that sometimes seem more unpalatable than they really are.

Teach me, Lord, not to expect more of myself than you do.

JUNE 25

Addictions

If you are not hooked on food, alcohol, or other drugs, then you have no addictions, right? Perhaps not. If only the list of addictions were limited to those few! But the addictions list also includes obsessions with work, and the uncontrollable urge always to be right. The list also contains such classics as anger, fear, lust, possessiveness, and the persistent desire to avoid effort. Even if no addiction on this list applies to you, there is a sure test that identifies whether or not you are really free. Here is the test. If you experience any harmful thought or action that you cannot adequately control, this signals the strong possibility that you may be hooked on something.

Addictions interfere with our freedom to live life peacefully. What peace can there be if we become our own tyrants? And what is it that can set us free from ourselves? Honesty, the frank admission of our own enslavement, would certainly be the first step. The humility to ask for help would be the second. And coupled with these steps would be an important belief: that there is a freedom-loving God who wants to help us achieve the freedom that is meant to be ours.

Help me to be honest, Lord, that I might discover those things that rob me of life and keep me from being free.

JUNE 26

The Offering

As Jesus sat near the Temple treasury, he watched the people as they dropped in their money. Many rich men dropped in a lot of money; then a poor widow came along and dropped in two little copper coins, worth about a penny. He called his disciples together and said to them, "I tell you that this poor widow put more in the offering box than all the others. For the others put in what they had to spare of their riches; but she, poor as she is, put in all she had — she gave all she had to live on."

— Mark 12:41–44

What a consolation! It does not take a lot of money or tremendous talent to create a worthwhile life. The widow gave hardly anything, but from another point of view, she gave far more than anyone else. The only thing necessary is to give fully of what you have, no matter how little. So there is never any reason to be envious of others' talents, even if they seem greater than your own. All that is required for greatness in life is to give fully of what has been given to you.

This is a consolation to me, Lord. Rightly or wrongly, I sometimes think that others are far more gifted than I. And now I see that it doesn't matter one way or another. What does matter is that I recognize my own gifts and give of them fully to those who need them. Help me to understand that this is how I become successful in your eyes.

JUNE 27

A Bad Joke

Several office workers decided to play a joke on a fellow employee. When the employee came to work, she was told, "Anne, you look sick. Don't you feel well?" This little scenario was repeated at least half a dozen times. Actually, Anne came to work feeling fine, but by the time her fellow employees finished with her, she went home feeling quite ill.

Some might think that Anne should have been made of tougher fiber. But the truth is that most of us are influenced, sometimes unconsciously, by what others say and do. In what way do we usually influence others? Do we build them up or tear them down? Do we help them to grow in self-esteem or do we put stumbling blocks in their way? When we intentionally influence the lives of others in a negative way, the harm we cause returns to its source and we ourselves become stunted. We remove ourselves from the climate of love that nourishes our own growth.

I may not often intentionally harm others, Lord, but I often ignore them. Instead of affirming others for the good they do and giving them the gift of hope, I pass them by without giving them anything at all. And I have done this to those who have had the greatest claim to my love. As you affirm me with your love, teach me to affirm others with mine.

J U N E 28

Remembering the Good

Once in a while, it is beneficial to think about the past. Otherwise, how can you profit from it? What happens when you think about your past? Probably, you can bring up a storehouse of positive and negative feelings, a flood of happy and sad events. All of those feelings and events have become a part of your life. The question is: which ones do you want to accentuate and hold on to?

People who cannot let go of the hurts and pains of the past rob themselves of the power to be joyful in the present. It is quite the opposite for those who accentuate the positive experiences of their past. They bring a hope to their lives that negative people find quite mysterious.

Positive and negative approaches to life eventually acquire the force of habit, but like most habits, we can either strengthen them or change them as we wish. Perhaps a good way to start is to remember some of the good things of the past that still linger as gifts in the present.

I am grateful, Lord, for all those who have loved me in my past, for the gift of that love still affects my present moment. I am grateful for all of your inspirations in my past, for they have helped to make me what I am at this moment. For all of the good remembrances, Lord, thank you.

JUNE 29

Wearing Out

Is it the burden we carry that wears us out, or are we finally worn out by the way we carry it? Resentments and anxieties increase the weight of any burden, and those problems come from the way we misuse our minds. Our minds can actually increase the sense of heaviness in our lives. And it is the misuse of our minds that wears us out, rather than the burdens we have to carry.

Jesus told us that our souls would find rest with him, because his yoke was easy and his burden light (Mt 11:29–30). Jesus' statement is true, so long as we do not complicate our lives by the misuse of our minds. It is the anxious and resentful mind that adds weight to burdens and wears us out before our time. Would humble trust in God lighten our burdens? Maybe so. That may be why Jesus invited us to take his yoke upon our shoulders and to learn from him, because he was gentle and humble of heart (Mt 11:29). It was only after he said this that he promised we would find the rest for which we so eagerly long.

Help me to think clearly about my life, Lord, to accept humbly those things that I really cannot change. May I not wear myself out with the negative thinking that will only make my burdens heavier.

J U N E 30

"I Am Who I Am"

When Moses asked God what his name was, God replied, "I am who I am" (Ex 3:14). That may not have enlightened Moses very much, but it did tell him all he needed to know. It was not necessary for Moses to know how God would carry out the promises he made, or how God would protect him and his people from harm. It was enough for Moses to know simply that God is who he is. If God is who he is, then everything else would certainly fall into place.

Can we be satisfied simply knowing that God is who he is? All of our hope is centered in this. It may not be clear how God will protect us, fulfill us, or save us, but if he is who he is, then nothing else matters. Just because God is God, he will bring meaning from apparent chaos, victory from what seems like defeat, life from the appearance of death. Because of his name, God cannot do otherwise. Our task is to accept him, to let God be God, and to trust in his name.

You are a mystery to me, God, but because you are God, because you are who you are, I will trust you. I wrap my life in the power of your name.

JULY

JULY 1

Lord, You Are Wonderful Indeed

"From now on all people will call me happy,
because of the great things the Mighty God
has done for me. His name is holy."

— Luke 1:48–49

With these words, Mary, the mother of Jesus, acknowledges all that God has done for her. There
is a simple matter-of-factness to her statement, for
she simply says what is true. Only someone who
is truly humble can make a statement like that.
And Mary was humble because she knew the great
things done for her were all gifts of God. Knowing
where the gifts came from, she was able to know
the truth about herself and to thank the source from
which her gifts came.

All of us can echo in our own lives what Mary
said about herself, for God has done great things

in all of us. He has given us life; he has given us our capabilities; he has given us our friends. God creates our greatness by endowing us with his love and life. Our gifts are so plentiful and obvious that we often forget them. When we forget, we can no longer make Mary's prayer our own, for her prayer comes from a deep consciousness of her own worth as a gift of God.

Let me see myself as you do, Lord Jesus, and help me to believe that what you see is precious in your eyes.

JULY 2

Impossibilities

God makes the impossible to be possible for us, not so much by changing what goes on outside of ourselves, but by helping us to change what goes on within. Strength to do what seems impossible comes from the God for whom all things are possible. It is the Spirit of God within us that tells us what is ultimately possible for us. In quiet reflection and trust we come to know what God wants us to do and to believe that he will work with us as we do it. Trusting in him, we receive the strength to do what needs to be done.

Difficult things often become impossible when we try to accomplish them by ourselves. Perhaps our own experience teaches us that those who try to manage their lives by themselves become the sources of their own failures.

My own false thinking creates my imagined impossibilities, Lord, but the irony is that your strength is already within me, ready to help me if I accept it. Increase my awareness of your love and presence in my life.

JULY 3

A One-Way Ticket

For our journey through life, we are given a one-way ticket. We cannot repeat the journey and we cannot return to the point from which we started. Since we cannot relive any moments from the past, it makes sense to do things right in the present. And yet, it is more than just a matter of doing things right.

If life is a one-way ticket, we cannot afford to be unconscious of the beauty and meaning of our present moment. When our present moment becomes the past, we cannot recapture what was lost by our lack of awareness. That is why every moment should be lived with eyes and ears opened wide. Knowing that we travel with a one-way ticket through life, we can train ourselves to be more conscious of each one of our moments as we live them. Then at the end of our earthly lives, we will know the joy of having lived them to the fullest.

In many ways, I am only half alive, Lord. Teach me to become more aware of my thoughts and feelings, more aware of things outside of me that I might live more deeply.

J U L Y 4

Independence

America is famous for its insistence on individual freedom, and Americans have paid a great price to preserve this gift. We owe deep appreciation for those who have handed on this gift to us. But while treasuring independence and individual freedom, we discover that there is no freedom without the recognition of limits. We are truly free not when we are rid of all personal boundaries, but when we adjust to the boundaries imposed by others who also have the right to freedom.

I cannot be fully free unless you are. For if I do not care about your freedom, I become the slave of my own selfishness. I can truly celebrate the joy of individual freedom when I treasure your freedom as deeply as I treasure my own.

Thank you, Lord, for my country's freedom as well as for my own. May my understanding and experience of my own freedom not result in the impoverishment of the rights of others, but in the preservation of the rights of all.

J U L Y 5

John the Baptist

John's clothes were made of camel's hair; he wore a leather belt around his waist, and his food was locusts and wild honey.

— Matthew 3:4

Perhaps John the Baptist would not have been someone with whom you could immediately identify, or someone you ordinarily would have invited to dinner. But he had an extraordinary role to play among his contemporaries. He was the one who pointed out Jesus to the people of his time, and because of this, he has been immortalized in the story of Jesus' life.

Grasshoppers aside, the story of John is meant to be our own. Through our baptism we are called to point out Jesus to our contemporaries. The values that emanate from our lives are meant to make him known, to make his message and his presence credible to others. How can that happen if his followers do not point him out by the way they live their lives? What John the Baptist began, we continue to carry out, so that Jesus might be known among the people with whom we live and work.

John did you a great service, Lord. Through your help, may I be able to do the same.

J U L Y 6

Hospitality

It may seem strange to think of God as offering us hospitality. But when he invited us into his world and into his very life by a magnificent act of creation, that is exactly what God did. His act of creation is an act of welcome, an act of hospitality that says to us, "I want you to share my life, and to allow me to share in yours. The universe is my home and I invite you into it. Enjoy it with me."

175

We return the hospitality of God when we invite him into our own lives, when we say "yes" to his request to be with us. Through the mutual offering and acceptance of hospitality, friendship and love grow.

The process completes itself when we imitate God by offering hospitality to one another. It is an offering that begets friendship, an offering that enhances the joy of life. Whenever we give hospitality to one another, we imitate the God who is constantly hospitable to us.

Forgive me for not understanding the meaning of your hospitality, Lord, and for my lack of thankfulness in not passing it on to others.

J U L Y 7

Belonging

Is happiness possible if you have no experience of belonging to anyone? The feeling of belonging entwines your life with others, and you come to experience something of your own meaning through the relatedness of love. The opposite would be loneliness, an experience of belonging to no one.

The ultimate meaning of religion is to experience our lives as belonging to God, to the God who passionately wants to belong to us. We already live and move and have our being in God, but the personal experience of this is what gives rise to the feeling of belonging. This experience is open to all of us, but, depending on our personalities and backgrounds, it comes in different ways. Some will discover the sense of belonging to God by means of a deep awareness of nature, others through the celebration of liturgy, still others through the experience of human love and caring. Many will discover their belonging to God through an awareness of their own inner life, for at the core of that life is God.

This sense of belonging to God comes gradually with our prayerful awareness of ourselves and of life around us. Those who seek passionately with perseverance, quiet prayer, and trust will discover the goal of their quest, because it is God's will to be known.

Lord, you created me so that you and I could belong to each other. Thank you. May I never alienate myself from you.

J U L Y 8

Experiencing for Yourself

When we were young, most of us had parents or teachers who told us what God is like. And when we read the Bible, we saw words describing how the first Christians experienced God. As we mature spiritually, we want to experience what God is like for ourselves. Others pointed the way for us, but they could do no more than point. They could not live our own experiences for us. We are the only ones who can do that for ourselves, and if we fail, then religion is merely a collection of other people's ideas. It ceases to become a personal dynamic force in our own lives.

God is real for us when our discovery of him becomes a personal experience. The more deeply we become prayerfully aware of the life within us and the life around us, the more personal our discovery of God becomes. The discovery is made any time we decide to become completely aware and awake in our present moment, for God reveals himself to us everywhere.

I am grateful for what others have told me of you, my God, but I need to experience you in the unfolding of my own life. I often forget to look for you, and when I do remember, I usually see you darkly, as if I were looking through a veil. May my understanding grow and my consciousness become more alert.

J U L Y 9

Unfairness

Life never seemed more unfair than when Jesus died on the cross. For a just man to be killed seems totally senseless. For Jesus to be killed seems absolutely incredible. His only desire was to reveal God's tremendous love. Perhaps the response he got would have been predictable, and if Jesus had come at another time in history, the response would probably have been similar. The mystery of human ignorance and evil is interwoven with life. It touches our own lives, and when it does, life seems unfair.

Perhaps much of life's apparent unfairness could be reduced if we were fairer to one another. If the people around Jesus would have truly decided to love, Jesus would not have died on the cross. If we decided to care for one another, some of life's unfairness would disappear for us too. Of course, this is an ideal. Not everyone is interested in making life fairer for others. But if we follow Christ, that must be our interest. And who would deny that, sometimes at least, we might reap the benefits of what we sow?

Lord, may I not add to the unfairness that is already so much a tragic part of life. May I bring the kind of love to the people around me that you brought, the kind of love that you still continue to bring.

J U L Y 10

Searching

Beware of those for whom life is a puzzle already solved, those for whom things are too clear. If you fall into this category, you may be on a dangerous path. If you already have the full and complete answers to all the important questions of life, there may be nothing left for you to learn. And if you are in a position of authority, you may be a serious stumbling block for others.

Our experience of any part of our lives can become fossilized when we think our picture of it is complete. A fossil is stuck with itself as it is. It cannot change and grow. The joy of being fully alive is the joy of being able to expand our minds through the willingness to discover something new, even when that threatens the security of long-cherished viewpoints.

People who search for truth with humble, open minds treat themselves to the possibility of wisdom and to the joy of expanding their horizons. It is a hard job at times, but consider the alternative. Who would want to become a fossil before his or her time?

I may know more than some people, Lord, but I'm not always sure who those people are. May my mind be a searching one, supple and open to learning, listening, and growing.

JULY 11

Dreaming

"I will pour out my spirit on everyone: your sons and daughters will proclaim my message; your old men will have dreams, and your young men will see visions."

— Joel 2:28

Take a few moments to imagine what you would really want your life to be like. Is there something in particular that you would desire to achieve, an experience you would want to have, or an attitude you would like to develop? Which people and what circumstances of your life would help you to achieve your dream? Which people and what circumstances would hinder you? What could you do about it?

Without dreams, very little in life is ever realized, because our dreams are the guides that make us to be what we are. When we stop dreaming, we snuff out the possibilities of the growth-producing experiences that form the richness of life. In fact, without dreams, we are already half dead. But can it be that God himself calls us to life by sometimes causing our most worthwhile fantasies?

Lord, I hope I never reach a point in my life where I no longer have dreams. May your spirit inspire my dreams, and may my dreams spur me on to become the person you have created me to be.

J U L Y 12

Tensions

Tensions are messages from our bodies. Sometimes they tell us that something is amiss in our lives. A person in the wrong line of work may develop tension headaches. People who carry grudges may develop ulcers. Fearful individuals or people who do not trust themselves may experience muscular tightness. The mind reflects its state of awareness on to the body, and the body reciprocates by doing the same thing to the mind. A vicious circle comes into being.

The process has a positive side for us if we are able to learn from it, but the process is wasted if we refuse to attend to its meaning. In that case, all we are left with is the pain. At times, it takes honest, creative thinking to link the tension with its cause. We need to look at the unsatisfactory side of our lives and admit the failed personal relationships, the failed dreams, the self-defeating attitudes that poison our lives. If we are able to make the link between those things and physical tensions, then we will have heard our body's message. When the

181

message is acknowledged and received, it no longer has a reason to stay with us. It goes away and leaves us in peace.

I know that tensions are my body's messages to me, Lord, but I need help in deciphering the messages' meaning. I need the courage to look honestly at myself, the humility to ask for help when I need it, and the ability to trust that you will have a part in my healing.

J U L Y 13

Television

If you are an average American, you may spend some time watching television this week. And if you watch the adventure stories or the situation comedies, you will eventually catch on to the common phenomenon that unites them all. Somehow, when the story ends, all the problems will have been successfully solved; everything will have turned out all right.

In one sense, this kind of solution is ultimately true to life. When we flow from this life into the next, everything will finally work out for those who believe in the power of God. That is the meaning of the resurrection which gives hope to our present moment.

In another sense, the television solutions are untrue to life. They give the idea that basic problems are most often worked out in the here and now. People who learn to expect that are often disappointed. The wise person works in this life without the sure expectation that his or her efforts will bear the expected fruit, but the uncertainty causes no wavering in the work. To work with love is worthwhile no matter what the outcome. Successes and apparent failures are all woven into the resurrection. This is what the Father did for his Son, Jesus. That is what he will do for us.

Jesus, give me the strength to work without undue concern for success, and to believe that through the resurrection, all the threads of my life will be brought into harmony and unity.

J U L Y 14

Maybe, Jesus

Nothing drains energy and joy faster than living a halfhearted life. The resurrected presence of Jesus touches our consciousness with friendship and power, but we never quite open ourselves fully to receive it. We are invited to a vibrant life of love and caring service, but we respond, "Maybe, Jesus. I'll test the waters. I'm not absolutely sure. I'll see how things turn out."

There is within us a deep-seated fear of fully committing ourselves to God. Maybe we are afraid of being cheated if we respond completely to the message and presence of Jesus. We seem to fear that trusting in Jesus will give us less fulfillment and security than trusting in ourselves. But we have experienced the results of not fully committing ourselves to the God who lovingly calls us in the depths of our hearts. Finally we have to decide for ourselves what is best for us: to endure the permanent unfulfillment of a half-committed life, or to pass through a temporary fear so that we can know the joy of a life fully committed to Christ.

You know my temerity, Jesus, and we both know the pain it has caused. Help me to be courageous and generous in loving you, so that my wavering may be put to rest.

JULY 15

Going Back

Elderly people are not the only ones who reminisce with fondness about the past. Sometimes when the present moment seems difficult and unfulfilling, the temptation is to think that things were better for us in times gone by. But even when the present looks bleak, would we really want to go back and experience our lives as they once were? Who would want to trade the knowledge and hard-won wisdom of life experience for the immaturities of the past?

Compare yourself now to what you were in the past. When you catch a glimpse of the spiritual and psychological growth that has become a part of you over time, you can be thankful for what you are at the present moment. And perhaps the best is yet to come!

Help me to see how my life has grown and evolved over time, Lord, so that I might be more content, and more grateful for the wisdom you have given me.

Witnessing

You can tell a person by the company he or she keeps. That is easily understood. People who are truly our friends affect us in positive ways and change us for the better. And since that influence becomes a part of us, it shines out in our relationships with others.

Friends of God should be able to notice some positive effects of their friendship. Their lives change, and even others notice the difference. They become witnesses to the love of God within them. I have met people like that in my life. Perhaps you have too. Such people are gifts that act like a leaven within the lives of others.

"Witness" is a biblical word used to describe a follower of Jesus. To be a witness means to follow Jesus out of love and to accept his words as true. It also means to attract other people to Jesus because of one's own love for him. Christian witnessing is a total, loving, and experiential following of Christ which radiates to others. Such a witness touches and changes human life in many wonderful ways. When people mutually witness to the love of God, his presence can be sensed in their midst, and through this experience, they come to know the meaning of the kingdom of God.

I ask earnestly, Lord, that my life might be a witness to your kingdom.

The Middle Road

Workaholics rarely experience the joys of leisure time, and leisure addicts rarely experience the joy of productive work. To miss out on either one is to deny oneself the feeling of psychological and spiritual equilibrium. That seems to be a part of the Genesis message which says that after God made human beings, he took a rest (Gn 2:2). Presupposing that the effort of creation did not tire him out, perhaps he took the rest so that he could enjoy what he had made.

If you are a workaholic or a leisure addict, do yourself a favor and broaden your awareness of some other areas of your life. Not only will you increase your zest for life and the quality of what you are doing (or not doing), but you will also increase the happiness of those around you.

The fuller joy in life is in the experience of traveling the middle road, avoiding the extremes. If you have found the middle road, you already know the joy of savoring a more complete experience of life. If you are searching for it, then you are on an adventure of which the best part is yet to come.

To experience only one side of life is to experience dullness. Lord, keep me from the extremes.

Grieving

No one who lives long enough escapes the experience of grief. Whenever we notice that a part of us is growing old, that an important relationship is in its death throes, or whenever anything meaningful is taken from us, we experience psychological pain. We walk continually with the possibility of loss. And sooner or later we grieve for what we actually lose.

The Bible tells us in many ways that a resurrection is always preceded by a death. And so we hope that grief will eventually be turned to joy, because behind every loss there will be a finding, and behind every death, a fulfillment. If we think back over our lives, sometimes this rings true. What we regarded as loss eventually turned into gain. Grieving was changed into joy. But at other times, we may not see this process at work. We wait for a meaning that may only appear when we pass from this incomplete life to the fuller one to come. All that we can do then is to trust, because we discover that there is nothing more meaningful that we can do.

Jesus, you and I have both grieved. As you trusted your Father, may I learn to trust. As you experienced resurrection, may I experience resurrection. And when I grieve, be a part of me with your strength and your compassion.

Fire

If you want to know the presence of God in your life, take a lesson from fire. Fire only unites itself to what it burns when it burns brightly and deeply. Otherwise, there is only smoke. In a similar way, you only come to know God when you burn for the experience of knowing him. Otherwise, you never see deeply.

Desire makes vision possible. God cannot show himself to you unless his revelation meets your desire. If there is no desire, there is no expectation, no state of being awake, no consciousness eager to receive the revelation.

The desire to know God is God's gift. But if the gift is not received with a wide-awake enthusiasm, the gift has no meaning for the one who receives it. God becomes real for us in proportion to the eagerness of our desire to discover him.

Lord, increase my desire to experience your presence. Pardon me for the disinterest that has kept me from finding you.

The Joy of Living

Some people have a hard time living joyfully. Rejection, poverty, a poor self-image, and fear are some of the experiences that dampen people's ardor for life. And yet there are many people living in terrible circumstances who, in spite of them, still exude a zest for living. How do they do it?

If you read about the life of Jesus, you know that he exuded a zest for living, a sense of joy. His basic message was about love. Would this have been the secret of his joy, of the spirit of life that he seemed to radiate to others? If that was his secret, we might tend to think that it would not work for us. Joyful, loving people certainly do not have our problems! And yet it is sometimes the people with the most difficult problems who are the most joyful. You and I have seen them. I have seen this joy in the poor and in the dying.

Does a certain joy of life come from knowing that you are loved by God, that you are secure in his hands, that you have worth, and that you have been genuinely loved by others? Does the joy increase when you give it away? And could that kind of joy be so strong that it could even shine through the clouds of physical and psychological suffering?

Lord, increase my consciousness of love and the zest that I so desire to feel for life. When I see people who are joyful, help me to discover their secret.

J U L Y 21

Watch Out!

Something out there is after you, and if you are not careful, it will catch you without your being aware that you were even caught. And what's after you? Well, what are some of the messages and attitudes that continually bombard you in your daily life? Violence, commercialism, excessive individualism, emphasis on irresponsible pleasure, cavalier attitudes toward honesty, these are a few of the suggestions that consistently pollute all of our lives. To what extent have you been influenced by them? Watch out! You may be partially hooked without knowing it. Only a thoroughly honest and wakeful conscience will ever know.

"Be alert, be on watch! Your enemy, the Devil, roams around like a roaring lion, looking for someone to devour. Be firm in your faith and resist him" (1 Pt 5:8–9). Our devils prowl among us in contemporary form. Have you been able to detect them and to resist?

Keep me watchful, Lord, that I may do nothing to mar my consciousness of your presence.

J U L Y 22

Heaven

Heaven is the fulfillment of life given by God through the resurrection, but few of us are in any hurry to receive the gift. Is that because reality beyond this life seems so obscure? But we already know something about heaven. We already know something about the life to come.

If you were to look at heaven simply as a place, then the idea of heaven may not make much sense. But suppose you were to look at it as a state of consciousness, as a total experience of loving and belonging to God and to all that he has made. You have probably already experienced something of this. Whenever you have experienced a sense of belonging to someone through a loving and caring relationship, whenever you have come more alive through a peaceful relatedness to God, whenever you have experienced a unity with nature, in all of those moments you have had a dim vision of heaven.

In this life, the vision is fleeting and unclear. But when you are freed from space and time through resurrection, then the sense of belonging will be complete. When you become fully conscious of absolute love and belonging, then you are in heaven. We already know something about it. But there is more to come.

Completeness of consciousness and complete-ness of belonging are your promise and gift to me, Lord. Thank you. May my awareness of this gift begin now.

J U L Y 23

Saints

Saints are the heroes of consciousness. They are men and women whose awareness of love and belonging penetrated everything they did. And so they appeared different from most of us, because they were more alive. It makes sense to honor them, because they are models of what human life can be like. They teach us what we ourselves can become.

Saints are loveable because they struggled with the same basic human problems and difficulties that we all do. We can relate to saints from that point of view, and we can relate to the imperfections that were a part of their lives, just as they are a part of ours. But the saints were willing to go beyond their imperfections and ego concerns, and that is what made them saints. Their love was apparent by the way they lived and served. Because of this, they teach us what we too can be.

The saints understood and used the gifts you gave them, Lord. Help me to understand and use mine.

JULY 24

Repent

"The right time has come," he said, "and the Kingdom of God is near! Turn away from your sins and believe the Good News!"
— Mark 1:15

Turning from sin could seem to mean that we are merely asked to give something up. But the original Greek word behind turning from sin was "metanoia" which meant to "go beyond the mind." The idea was to go beyond one's ego, to go beyond one's ordinary way of experiencing life and, instead, to expand one's mind, to become God-centered.

Everything a person does with his or her life depends on "going beyond the mind," going beyond the usual way in which he or she experiences life. What one finally does with his or her life depends on where the mind is. If the mind broadens itself so that it knows God's embrace, then its acts will be God-like. This is what turning from sin does.

It lifts one's life from fragmentation to the integrity that comes when one chooses to be with the God who loves.

I've never really understood the meaning of turning from sin, Lord. I need to understand it in its broader meaning. May I turn from sin by growing out of my ordinary state of consciousness to the awareness of your presence and love.

J U L Y 25

You Are Gods

"It is written in your own Law that God said, 'You are gods.'"

— John 10:34

Through the incarnation of Jesus, the Son of God became like us, sharing in our human nature. The incarnation also has another consequence. Through the birth of Jesus, we are destined to be like God, sharing in his divine nature.

Jesus tells us that we are treasured by God, and that if we accept God's love we become like God who is love. When we become like God, we experience salvation, a term that signifies the wholeness that is ours when we are wholly one with love. We become conscious of wholeness through prayerful communication with God and through caring relationships with others. The more we experience and live out our oneness with others, the more we become like God. Jesus incarnated himself to

193

announce this truth, and to empower us to incarnate his presence among those whose lives we touch.

Jesus, you have shown me what I am to become. You have invited me to become like you. In my wildest dreams, I would never have imagined anything like this. I still don't quite grasp it, Lord. Be patient with my dullness.

J U L Y 26

20/20

Not many people can claim the perfection of 20/20 vision. For those lucky enough to have it, things both near and far can be seen with effortless clarity. For most of us who do not have it, our vision with the naked eye is somewhat skewed.

We use the word "see" to apply not only to physical vision, but to spiritual and psychological vision as well. Skewed seeing happens on these levels too. How many people can claim 20/20 vision in their spiritual and psychological views of life? But when that kind of vision becomes skewed, what is the corrective?

We know skewed psychological and spiritual vision by the pain it causes. If a particular outlook on life causes pain, we can at least be aware of the possibility of changing it. We can examine the various possibilities of change and choose one that would seem more satisfying. Since the choice might initially be a difficult one, we could decide to ask God's power to help us make it. And if the changed psychological or spiritual vision brought us peace, then we would know that the choice was a sensible one. The procedure seems reasonable and yet it is often difficult to follow. Why is it that we so often prefer our skewed outlooks to their healthier alternatives?

I don't always associate my dissatisfactions with my skewed outlooks on life, Lord. It seems easier to blame my dissatisfactions and failures on others. Help me to bring my life into focus, to have the 20/20 vision that will help me to see what is true.

J U L Y 27

Evenness of Mind

Our ability to accept all things, not only our joys but also the sorrows we cannot change, is what finally gives birth to evenness of mind. A person with an even mind accepts the unlovable with the loveable, the disagreeable with the agreeable, without allowing himself to be disturbed and unbalanced.

A sense of equilibrium comes from accepting the painful aspects of our lives that are simply a part of everyone's life. Peace begins when we permit ourselves to admit and experience our fears, guilt, frustrations, and losses, accepting things as they are and not as we think they should be. Changing what we can, and accepting what we cannot, a sense of evenmindedness grows in us that gives birth to peace. No longer fighting life, we flow with it. And somehow, we discover that it becomes our friend.

Evenmindedness seems like a miracle, Lord, but I won't have peace until this miracle becomes a part of me. Grant me the wisdom to accept the dark side of my life, to accept all those things in my life that I can't change. But give me the strength to change what I can.

J U L Y 28

Ebb and Flow

When our hearts hurt and our spirits sag, we need something to make us feel alive again. That "something" is different for each of us. At some point, we feel a need to renew our vitality in our own way. Isn't every life marked by an ebb and flow of enthusiasm and energy? When enthusiasm and energy decrease, there is something that can be done to revive them.

Some of us are quite poor at taking care of ourselves, or giving ourselves what we need to experience more fully the goodness of life. Within the possibilities of our life circumstances, we need to be good to ourselves. We need to allow time for quiet in the midst of noise, time for ourselves in the midst of caring for others, time to do something we like in the midst of fulfilling our responsibilities. How good a job we do in caring for ourselves influences our experience of the ebb and flow of life. If there are too many "ebbs," something may be amiss.

I don't serve you well, Lord, if I ignore my own legitimate needs. May I learn from the ebb and flow of my life how to care appropriately for myself.

JULY 29

Imagining God

If you were to paint a picture of God, what would God look like? Would God have a kind face or a stern one? Would God look like a judge? Or would you choose the gospel portrayal of a smiling, compassionate preacher with arms outstretched, inviting you to come close with joy?

The way you picture God to yourself determines how you let God become a part of your life. You may not expect too much from a stern-faced judge. Some years ago, a letter to the editor appeared in a popular magazine with this question: "Why is it that religion always takes the fun out of life?" One wonders how the writer pictured God.

Perhaps one of the most beautiful "pictures" of God can be found in John, chapters 14–17. If we can believe that God is as tender and caring as these chapters say, then we have cause for much hope and love. Is your picture of God anything like the self-portrait God "paints" in the Bible?

Help me to change any false ideas I may have of you, Jesus. Help me to see you and to accept you as you are.

Learning From Sin

Sin has been defined as an act that misses the mark. Metaphorically, the sinner's action is like an arrow that fails to reach its destination. Because it never gets to the place where it is supposed to be, it is useless. Even though the sinful act is useless in itself and often tragic, it does have the power to teach.

Sin, or missing the mark, always teaches us something about ourselves. It teaches us about our weaknesses, but also about the forgiving power of God who lifts us up whenever we allow ourselves to be touched by him. Sin also says something about our own personalities and even something about the society in which we live. The struggle to overcome sin teaches us even more about ourselves, making us aware of where our strengths lie. Sin teaches us who our enemies are, but eventually, it also points out those who are our allies.

It is a waste of time to sin, but if we finally come to learn something from it, then we allow God to "write straight with the crooked lines" of our lives.

I'm sorry for the times I've missed the mark, Lord, but may I at least learn something from my poor aim.

Growing

When we grew into adolescence from childhood, people saw that we had changed. Our childish appearance died, but what was essential in us continued to live. When we grew into adulthood from adolescence, people saw that we had changed. Our adolescent appearance died, but what was essential in us continued to live. When we grow into the next life from this one, people will see that we have changed. Our earthly appearance will have died, but we will continue to live. Death is simply part of the continuum of growth and life.

People do not always grow gracefully. Sometimes they want to hang on to childhood or to adolescence instead of joyfully entering the next stage of life. And many times they want to hang on to this life instead of joyfully entering the next. Those who flow with the movement of life will avoid hanging on to any particular stage. They will simply go where the growth of life carries them, letting go of what was and embracing what is to come.

I try to believe that life is growth, Lord, and that what I call death is simply part of the process of the total growth of life. Give me the courage to leave the past, and to embrace with vibrant anticipation what is yet to come.

AUGUST

AUGUST 1

Sculpture

A sculptor sees a block of marble and envisions the latent possibilities within it. Slowly and carefully, he chips away at the marble, and gradually its possibilities begin to take shape. Finally, his persevering artistry produces a magnificent piece of work that brings joy not only to himself, but also to others.

Something similar happens when a person looks at her life with the eyes of a sculptor. She sees the latent possibilities. Slowly and carefully, whatever blocks out the chosen image is chipped away. Finally, the persevering love produces a polished personality that brings joy not only to the individual herself, but also to others.

If our lives sometimes seem like blocks of marble, we need the artistic intuition to see the latent possibilities within ourselves that we can bring to life.

You have created me with latent possibilities that reflect something of your own image, Lord. May I chip away at the selfishness that keeps the image from taking shape.

A U G U S T 2

Leave Us

When Jesus came to the territory of Gadara on the other side of the lake, he was met by two men who came out of the burial caves there. These men had demons in them and were so fierce that no one dared travel on that road. At once they screamed, "What do you want with us, you Son of God? Have you come to punish us before the right time?"

Not far away there was a large herd of pigs feeding. So the demons begged Jesus, "If you are going to drive us out, send us into that herd of pigs."

— Matthew 8:28–31

That is precisely what Jesus did, but when the townspeople heard about it, they asked him to leave. This seems to be a case of greater sympathy for pigs than for the healing presence of Jesus. In those times when the presence of Jesus has disconcerted us and forced us to a choice, how have we chosen? Has our choice for secondary and un-worthy goals sometimes prompted us to ask Jesus to leave us?

Lord, pardon me for those times when I have allowed myself to feel inconvenienced or embarrassed by you, and for those times when I've pushed you away.

AUGUST 3

Famine

The lack of food and water is a cause of much suffering in many parts of the world. In our part of the world, most of us are fortunate, because our problem is quite different. We struggle to avoid eating too much. Yet, because of our abundance, we may experience famine of another sort.

A person untouched by the sufferings of others experiences famine of the spirit. When love and compassion are in short supply, the inner spirit of a person begins to die. Left only with his or her concerns for self, such a person is left without the nourishment that comes from caring about others.

The results of famine of the spirit perpetuate themselves, because one person's lack of concern adversely touches the lives of others in many different ways.

Lord, may I avoid the callousness that causes so much of the spiritual and material famine in my brothers and sisters.

Symbols

Some kinds of reality can only be known through symbols. We would never be conscious of human love unless it expressed itself through words and gestures. Its words and gestures are the symbols through which human love tells us about itself.

We would never know God unless he expressed himself through his creation and through his words. These are God's symbols. They point to the ultimate reality who communicates himself through them. The more attentive one is to these symbols, the more one discovers the reality to which they point. A good symbol reader learns to understand the symbolic language of God, and in deciphering the language, he discovers something of the mystery of God's presence in the world.

The symbols of your love and presence pervade my life abundantly, Lord. May I be awake to them so that I might read the message you give through them. May the symbols become transparent for me so that I might decipher their meaning.

Boredom

Imagine a child sitting in the midst of a huge pile of toys and saying to his mother, "Mom, there's nothing to do." In a similar way, a kind of boredom strikes us when we become saturated with the stimulating realities surrounding our lives. The richness of life becomes so ordinary to our consciousness that we cease being aware of it. The resulting ennui makes us tired of our commitments, perhaps even tired of life itself.

You can make the ordinary realities in life become extraordinary only when you learn to see them anew. That will never happen unless you open your eyes and pay attention to the people and to the surroundings that are a part of your life. When you do that with some diligence, you begin to see in a fresh way. Perhaps no one can fully explain how this process works, but then that is not really necessary. The only thing necessary is to look with the careful attention that eventually enables all of us to break through the ordinariness of our lives.

When I start to get bored, God, teach me to open my eyes.

AUGUST 6

Opening Up

If God seems far away from you, ask yourself if you have given him the opportunity to come close. Is there something in you that prevents you from opening up to his presence?

Opening up to God's presence begins with the belief that you are loved, that God actually takes a delight in being with you. Opening up to God would mean to admit your faults and failures, to ask pardon for them and to believe that you are loved in spite of them. Opening up to God's presence would include an awareness that he is already within you, within everyone and everything that surrounds you, and that he waits for you to make this discovery.

Our opening up to God makes his closeness apparent to us. The experience begins whenever we make the decision to allow it to happen.

The next time you seem far away, Lord, I'll ask myself how open I am to receive you. And if I can find no cause in myself for your apparent absence, then I will simply believe that you are with me in the darkness.

A U G U S T 7

Heads or Tails?

"Tails" is just as much a part of a coin as "heads." It is the same coin either way, and although heads and tails are opposites, you could not imagine a coin without both of them.

The heads and tails of a coin resemble a curious fact about our lives. Joys and sorrows are the heads and tails of life, and it would be hard to imagine a life in which both of them were not present. Both joys and sorrows teach us something if we reflect on their meaning. Rather than trying to escape unavoidable sorrows, we might simply let them be our instructors, flowing with the pattern of opposites that both sorrows and joys produce in our lives.

My usual posture toward unavoidable sorrows is to try to avoid them, or to rebel against them, Lord. Much of the meaning of sorrow must remain a mystery for me, and yet I know that sorrow is an integral part of life. Teach me to accept what cannot be changed, and to learn from my life as it is.

AUGUST 8

Pretensions

It seems less risky at times to show a false front to others than it is to let them see who we really are. But if we do that, how will we ever know whether we are loved for our real selves or for our masks?

It seems less risky at times to hide our faults from God than it is to face him as we really are. But if we do that, how will we ever know God's unconditional love and his compassionate forgiveness?

It may seem that our pretenses keep us from experiencing painful rejections, but in reality, they only keep us from knowing ourselves and from being truly loved. Losing out on those experiences is far more painful than taking the risk of removing our masks.

You taught us, Jesus, that you love us unconditionally as we are. Those who are truly my friends will love me in the same way. May I have the courage not to worry about those who cannot love me for who I am.

Restoration

Coming back to a friendship that has been broken is a painful process. Maybe that is why it takes time to build up the courage to restore a broken relationship. We need to be patient with ourselves and with those who struggle for the humility to mend what has been fractured.

Even after the first steps toward reconciliation and restoration are made, the rebuilding of trust involves discipline, and the process is not without its pain. Old habits of selfishness are hard to break. We know that from the times we have tried to restore friendship with those we have hurt. And we know that from the times we have tried to restore friendship with God.

As painful as the process of restoring divine and human relationships might be, it is even more painful to remain alienated from God and removed from those we love. Love finally compels us to try to restore bonds that have been broken, and if the love is mutually nurtured, its healed bonds will grow in strength.

Lord, may I not be too proud or too afraid to restore any of my broken relationships to whatever degree I can.

AUGUST 10

Lures

To catch the attention of a small child, you might try offering an interesting toy or a piece of candy. To catch the attention of a worldly person, you might try offering flattery or money. When God wants to catch our attention, what does he use?

God, of course, is a master at capturing human attention. He uses the lure of human love that reflects his own presence in our midst. He uses the lure of sunsets, oceans, and stars, or whatever it is in nature that makes our own personalities come alive and take notice of what he has made. God uses the lure of our own inner peace which comes when he floods a particular moment of our lives with his presence. Because God's imagination is infinite, the lures he uses to attract our attention are many. There is never a problem with a lack of lures, but there may be a problem with our lack of awareness of them.

It's your love, Lord, that impelled you to create the many lures in this world that attract me to you. May my love impel me to notice them.

AUGUST 11

Alienation

A feeling of being out of touch, a sense of being disconnected from others, an experience of disequilibrium within ourselves: these are the hallmarks of alienation, a painful sensation that sometimes clouds our lives. If it happens to you, know that you are not alone. An occasional experience of alienation is a part of life that touches all of us at times. But there may be something you can do to alleviate its painfulness.

Relax yourself and calmly pay attention to the rhythm of your breathing. Doing this simple exercise for a short period of time can foster a feeling of equilibrium. As you become more peaceful, it is easier to discover the reasons for the sense of alienation and to deal with its causes. If you are honest with yourself, you can often discover the reasons. If you cannot make the discovery by yourself, then you need to make it with someone qualified to help you. Reaching out for help is the price you pay for the insights that bring peace and healing.

Feelings of alienation tell us that something is wrong with our lives. In this sense, they are spurs to growth. When we get the message, the feelings of alienation diminish, and the new insights that become a part of us give birth to renewed peace and well-being.

Lord, I cause my sense of alienation by the way I look at my life. May I learn something from the pain caused by my mistaken vision.

A U G U S T 12

Apostles

We remember Jesus' apostles with gratitude because it was through their faith that the word of Jesus has come down to us. According to our own circumstances of life, we are meant to continue their ministry among those with whom we live and work.

Think back in your life to the people who handed on Christian faith to you by the way they lived. The message of Jesus is spread not only by preaching, but also by the lives of those who have heard the message and been changed by it. We see them, and we come to know how powerful and beautiful the word of God really is. When our lives are changed by the word, then others come to see the power and beauty of the word in us. If this is what we reflect to others, then our lives will have been successful beyond measure.

In my own way, Lord, I want to share in the ministry of your apostles. Use my life in any way you wish, so that it may reflect your presence among the people with whom I live and work.

A U G U S T 13

Repression

When unwholesome thoughts push their way into our minds, we often push them out by repressing them, by denying their existence and shoving them down into our unconscious. Unfortunately, the procedure never works because our unwholesome thoughts do not take kindly to being ignored. They grab at our minds until we acknowledge them and give them some attention. And so, if we want to rid ourselves of them, that is what we have to do.

Acknowledging unwholesome thoughts does not mean entertaining them or dwelling on them. It simply means admitting to ourselves that they are within us. We can do this without being frightened or perturbed by them. If there is no fear or perturbation, there is no repression, and if there is no repression, the power of unwholesome thoughts is weakened.

It is unhealthy not to acknowledge your troublesome thoughts, and if they come frequently, you might try to discover with a spiritual guide why that happens. By acknowledging the presence of what is troublesome to you, you will gradually become more free.

Teach me not to be afraid of what is unwholesome, Lord, but to acknowledge it calmly and honestly that I might gain freedom of mind.

A U G U S T 14

Signs

Then some teachers of the Law and some Pharisees spoke up. "Teacher," they said, "we want to see you perform a miracle."

"How evil and godless are the people of this day!" Jesus exclaimed. "You ask me for a miracle? No! The only miracle you will be given is the miracle of the prophet Jonah."

— Matthew 12:38–39

No other miracles or signs will be given except the sign of Jonah. Why? Perhaps Jesus had already given enough signs. Perhaps the lives of his followers were expected to be the miracles and signs pointing to the efficacy of God's message. In that case, no other signs would be needed.

Goodness in the world is a sign of the power of God's presence, but the sign only comes from those who allow themselves to be changed by God's power. When others notice the change, they are faced with the most compelling sign of all, for then they are confronted with a choice: either to accept the power of God who can also form their lives anew, or to reject that power and live only for themselves.

Lord, may I be more attentive to the signs of goodness in the people around me. May my own life be a sign of your loving power.

A U G U S T 15

Three Things

The prophet Micah said that the Lord has told us what he requires of us: to do what is right, to love goodness, and to live humbly with our God (Mi 6:8).

What a grand blueprint for human life. If you spend time with a friend today or help someone who needs you, you will have fulfilled the first part of the blueprint. If you notice the beauty of something God has made, or appreciate the goodness of someone who touches your life today, then you will have fulfilled the second part. And if you acknowledge that the strength to live your life this day is a free gift that comes to you from God, then you will have accomplished the third part.

What the prophet Micah offers us is a plan for a successful day. It includes the offering of care, being aware of the beauty of life, and trustfully relying upon God. Whoever does these things invites joy into his or her life and becomes a source of joy for others.

Keep me awake, Lord, to the opportunities of accomplishing this threefold plan in my life. May I not sleep through the occasions that challenge me to serve and to be conscious of your presence.

AUGUST 16

Self-Love

We were always told that self-love is a terrible thing, and yet Jesus told us that the love of ourselves should be the measure by which we love our neighbors (Lk 10:25–37). Could it be that there are both good and bad kinds of self-love?

It would seem to be a mark of ingratitude if we did not appreciate and love the personality God gave us, along with all the gifts and talents that make us to be who we are. If we could appreciate and love ourselves in this way, realizing that all we have comes from the creative hands of God, we would feel less nervous and more at peace with ourselves. This kind of self-love honors God and acknowledges the truth of our essential goodness.

On the other hand, we miss the truth about ourselves when we regard ourselves as better than others, or when we imagine that God has nothing to do with our genuine successes in life. This kind of self-love dishonors God and falsifies the reality of who we are.

True self-love leads to joyful, humble gratitude for the gift of our lives, and when we treasure ourselves appropriately, we acquire the ability to treasure the lives of others.

If you love me, Lord, it is only fitting that I love myself. May my love of self always be a love permeated with gratitude, and may it be the measure of my love for my neighbor.

A U G U S T 17

Broken Cisterns

"My people have committed two sins: they have turned away from me, the spring of fresh water, and they have dug cisterns, cracked cisterns that can hold no water at all."

— Jeremiah 2:13

It seems tragically logical. Whenever people lose sight of God, they always try to find a substitute. But since the substitute is never fully satisfying, it is like a broken cistern that cannot contain any life-giving joy.

St. Augustine echoed the thought of Jeremiah when he said that the human heart is restless until it rests in God. Sooner or later we experience this reality, but sometimes it takes a while for us to admit its truth. Perhaps we are afraid that, in having God, we will lose everything else that we hold of value. And so we build broken cisterns. Jesus told us that nothing would be lost if we took the risk of choosing God's kingdom first. He said to us, "Instead, be concerned with his kingdom, and he will provide you with these things" (Lk 12:31).

I, too, have dug cisterns that eventually broke, Lord, and it took me a while to admit that my digging had left me empty. But now I choose your life-giving presence, and I believe that whatever else is necessary will be given besides.

A U G U S T 18

The Union of Opposites

Weddings are joyful signs of two individuals who decide to unite as one. The partners retain their individual identities, but at the same time they experience the oneness of their love. A wedding is a union of opposites in life, individuality with oneness, man with woman.

Our life with God is something like a union of opposites, a union in which the infinite unites with the finite. There is the ecstasy of oneness, but without the blurring of the individuality which makes self-giving impossible.

The maturation of our inner life is something like a union of opposites, for when we understand how to integrate opposite feelings and attitudes, we experience a sense of unity and wholeness within ourselves. A person growing toward his or her wholeness knows how to integrate mercy and justice, joy and sorrow, work and leisure, confrontation and retreat. Nothing good is left out. Nothing is ignored or suppressed.

Lord, may I understand how to bring all the opposites of my life into harmony.

God's Love

While it is important that we love God, it is far more important that God loves us. If he did not love us first, we would not be able to love at all. In everything, the primacy is his, and without him we can do nothing. That is why he is like the parent, and we are like the children dependent upon the parent's continual creative love. If God were to stop his love, we would cease to be. We live only because God continually loves us into being.

God's interest in us is unconditional and unflagging, because that is simply the way God is. That is what it means for God to be God. There is nothing we can do to eradicate God's love for us, for if we were capable of that, we would be capable of eradicating God. Of course, we may not quite understand this kind of love, but such was the revelation of Jesus. When we finally accept this incredible largesse, we know that we rest secure in a love that at all times permeates every part of our being and every circumstance of our lives.

I bow down in adoration before you, Lord, because of the wonderfulness of who you are. But then you raise me to my feet and empower me to do what you do, to be in some way as you are. Without your unconditional love, I quite literally would have no existence at all.

AUGUST 20

Idols

My children, keep yourselves safe from false gods!

— 1 John 5:21

We worship no wooden idols and we adore no plaster deities. We are too sophisticated for that. Where then are our false gods to be found?

Idols are like black holes that fatally engulf anything that falls under the spell of their gravitational attraction. We know our idols by the way they engulf our time and energy, by the way they attract the focus of our consciousness and hold it captive. The more central our idols become in our minds, the more they take the place of God. That is why an idol is always such a dangerous reality. It destroys our chance for real happiness.

Idols come in different shapes and forms. They might be persons, or they might be material objects, but no matter what they are, we would know them by their effects. When we become possessive, when we think we cannot live without a certain person

218

or a certain thing, we have enslaved ourselves to an idol.

Fortunately, the experience of enslavement to idols always carries with it the possibility of deliverance. Eventually, every idol disappoints us, and when we catch on to this truth, we find that what enslaved us was really nothing at all. At that point, the fatal attraction dies and we become free.

Lord, may I become aware of my idols and free myself from their fatal attractions.

A U G U S T   21

Competition

When we do not feel accepted, we feel an urge to assert ourselves in order to experience a sense of self-worth. How much energy is lost from the effort of constantly having to build a self-image! And since the image we build is never quite good enough, we find ourselves in a vicious circle of competition. Even our games become arenas where we have to prove ourselves. We can tell the difference between a game that is played for fun and a game that turns into the deadly serious business of protecting our self-images.

A person who experiences the joy of being unconditionally accepted has no self-image that needs to be protected. He has no need to compete simply to assert his own self-worth. And so the person who is accepted unconditionally can live his life without tension. He can do his work, play his games, and live his life with a sense of freedom. When there is nothing to be proved, one can be at peace with life.

I don't have to prove my self-worth, for I always have your acceptance, Lord.

AUGUST 22

Flaws

Is it true, sometimes, that people's imperfections make them more lovable? Perhaps that depends on the type of imperfections involved. In any case, it would seem that those who are the most free are those who love others, and even life itself, in spite of its inescapable flaws.

Those who get stuck in the flaws are never free to love. When people pay more attention to the flaws of life rather than to its essential goodness, they become captives of their own flawed vision.

When you see the goodness of others shine through their imperfections, and the beauty of life radiate through its flaws, you see what many others miss. And if you have ever loved deeply, you will know what that statement means.

Teach me to look beyond life's imperfections, Lord, that I might see its essential goodness. Let me start with the ordinary events of this day, and with the people who in various ways are a part of my life.

AUGUST 23

Complacency

When things go well, we usually feel proud of ourselves. In conflict-free situations where it is easy to do the right thing, we might even feel a tinge of smugness about our virtue. It is a temptation to become complacent when things are easy for us, or when we think our goodness is due to the gift-edness of our own personalities. But how would things turn out if we were subjected to a severe trial? And how could we hope to come through that without the power of God?

If the day is easy and goes smoothly for you, give thanks that you have not been put to the test. Allow your God to walk with you in the easy days, so that when difficult ones come, he will not seem like a stranger to you. Then you will avoid the embarrassment that comes to those who only approach God when they are in dire need.

During the easy times of my life, Lord, may I neither be complacent nor take you for granted; for everything I have comes from you.

A U G U S T 24

Shadows

In the early morning, a tree casts a long shadow that covers everything in its path. As the sun rises higher, the shadow shortens, and when the sun is directly above the tree, there is no shadow at all. It projects no darkness. The tree and its surroundings are bathed in light.

Something similar happens to us as the light of consciousness takes greater hold of our minds. At first, we project our shadows and faults outside of ourselves on to others. As we become more conscious, we stop the projecting, realizing that our shadows and faults are really parts of ourselves. Through the light given us by the Spirit of God, we come to see ourselves and accept ourselves as we are, knowing that we are loved always. This self-knowledge enables us to integrate and heal within ourselves what we formerly projected on to others. Through the light of our honesty, we become whole.

Lord, I've often denied my faults and projected them on to others. In your light, may I admit the truth about myself, that I might take responsibility for my faults and be healed.

Religion

Is religion primarily a matter of behavioral laws and regulations, and primarily a matter of systematically defined creeds? If people are not led by the regulations and creeds to an experience of the living God, then they will have missed the true meaning of religion.

Religion in its deepest sense is a relationship between God and human beings, an awareness that couples intelligent creatures with their creator. Anything less than this chills people's love for religion, robbing them of its fruit and leaving them only with its outer skin. Of course, the outer skin is important because it protects the fruit, but why is it that some of us never get beyond the skin to taste the fruit within?

It's not surprising, Lord, that I've been bored by religion, because there are times when I haven't gotten beyond its peeling to taste the fruit. May your Spirit lead me deeper into awareness of your presence, so that I might discover what religion truly means.

AUGUST 26

Meaning What You Say

Words spoken without meaning touch no one's heart, neither God's nor man's. Would such words be best unspoken?

We speak meaninglessly whenever we speak mindlessly. Whenever we ask, "How are you?" without mindfulness or caring, we betray our lack of attention. And when we speak to anyone without attention, we show a lack of love.

Communication that touches the heart can be made only by those who are attentive to the persons they address, and who are mindful of what they say.

Lord, may I be awake and attentive to the way I communicate, and truly mean the words I speak.

AUGUST 27

Gentleness

The term "gentleness" conveys the ideal attitude that should permeate human relationships. Gentle people are strong, but their strength is never over-bearing. They are tolerant, but convinced of their own principles. They are able to show mercy while retaining a sense of justice. They are able to stand for their principles without forgetting kindness.

We should be as gentle as possible with others, because gentleness is what we would want others to show toward us. Above all, gentleness is what we would want God to show toward us, and we know from scripture that our God is a gentle God who knows how to temper justice with mercy. In being gentle with one another, we imitate God whose kindness graciously covers each one of us.

Jesus, may I be gentle with others as you have been gentle with me.

AUGUST 28

Wisdom

Wisdom is the ability to see things as they are, and the ability to respond to reality as it is. The wise person knows how to accept those things in life that cannot be changed, and how to try to change those things that need to be improved. The wise person knows how to relate to others in ways that would be best for them, treating all people according to their needs. The wise person also knows that the strength to do this comes not from himself or herself, but from God.

No fruitful human relationships are possible without wisdom, which is another word for mature love. Do you possess wisdom? You will come to know that by the growth of peace in your heart.

Lord, may I come to see things as they are and respond to reality as it is, relating to others in ways that are best for them.

AUGUST 29

When Nothing Happens

Sitting or walking with God day after day, we come to expect that a great expansion of spiritual awareness should be our reward. So often, however, nothing seems to happen. Sometimes we wonder if the effort is worth it. Could there be a better way for us to spend our time?

Prayer is something of a paradox. Sometimes, nothing seems to happen during our time of quiet prayer, but the effects of it are felt in different ways during the rest of the day. You can prove this by remembering the times when you stopped spending quiet periods with God. The more protracted the omission, the less peaceful your days became. Although it is hard to put this into words, you knew that something was missing in your life, that something had changed for the worse.

If we want the peace of God, we have to sit with him in what seems like darkness. The sitting is never a waste of time. Something happens in the sitting, and it often happens below the level of our conscious awareness. God works in the apparent darkness, and he slowly changes us as we live out our day. We have to trust his workings.

Lord, may I never be discouraged when I spend quiet time with you and nothing seems to happen. No time spent with you is ever wasted. You are the one who determines the ultimate fruit of my prayer. My part is simply to be with you in trust.

A U G U S T 30

How to Keep the Guitar in Tune

Guitars are nothing without their strings, although at times some guitars might be better off without them. But in the hands of a good player, a tuned guitar can be a thing of joy. Of course, there is an art to getting the guitar strings in tune. If they are too loose, all you get is a dull "thunk." If they are too tight, they may snap at the touch of a finger. So the trick is to regulate the tension of the strings between the two extremes.

Perhaps there is something for us to learn from the way the guitar stays in tune. We survive better if we can avoid extremes. Otherwise we get out of tune with ourselves and with others. Extremes are destructive, as we may well know from our own lives.

Life is full of polarities: naive optimism and melancholy pessimism; addiction to activity and addiction to sloth; exaggerated emotions and deadness of feeling; constant change and no change at all. You can add your own polarities to the list. If you cannot find your balance between them, your life may be somewhat like an out-of-tune guitar. If there is no sparkle or resilience in your life, check to see if your polarities are balanced and in tune.

Lord, help me to keep my spiritual and psycho-
logical equilibrium. When I'm off-center, help
me to recover a sense of balance.

To Be or Not to Be

There is something to be learned from bees. Each
bee has a particular task important to the entire
colony. The queen bee spends the day laying hun-
dreds of eggs. The worker bees gather nectar that
will be turned into honey. Other workers function
as air conditioners, furiously beating their wings to
keep the hive cool. Finally, there are soldier bees
who guard the hive's entrance in order to protect
the honey supply. They all work together for their
common survival.

God made bees to be just the way they are.
Queens, workers, and soldiers always function as a
team because of instinct. They have no choice. But
what if God had given bees the power of choice?
What if the queen bee could decide not to lay eggs,
or the workers and soldiers decide not to do their
jobs? The hive would die.

God made each of us according to the plan
he had for us. He gave us gifts and talents for the
good of others and even for our own enjoyment.
But what if we decided not to be the persons he
made us to be; not to use the talents he gave us to
use? What if we became unappreciative of our own
gifts? How would that affect our families and communities? How would our own personal happiness
be affected?

Lord, I accept the talents you have given me, along with their obligations. May I never refuse to become what you have made me to be, nor forget that my gifts have been given not just for myself, but also for the sake of others.

SEPTEMBER

SEPTEMBER 1

Work

You are fortunate indeed if you have work that brings you satisfaction, work that energizes you and gives you a sense of wholeness. If this is not what you experience in your job, your real work might be a volunteer activity that helps you to realize your creative gifts. In any case, if you have a task on which you can meaningfully focus your energies, you have a real cause for thankfulness.

In addition to being thankful for our own work, we can also be thankful for the work of others, for those who have built our homes, for those who have constructed our roadways, for those whose daily labor keeps our cities running, for those whose work nourished us when we were children. We have all relied heavily on the work of others, and its benefits come down to us each day of our lives.

Lord, thank you for enabling me to work and to find fulfillment in tasks that benefit other people. May I appreciate more deeply what I am able to do, and be thankful for the benefits that I have received from the work of others.

SEPTEMBER 2

Freshness

A room becomes stuffy and uninviting when its doors and windows are rarely opened. Because it remains closed, the air within it turns stale. Something similar happens to people when they become closed in upon themselves. Their excessive self-preoccupation causes inner stagnancy. It destroys their freshness of spirit.

People who open the doors of their lives to the presence and needs of others are able to experience life with a fresh perspective. Their consciousness is freed from being paralyzed by their own personal concerns, and they discover a freedom that allows them to expend more energy in the service of others. As their self-preoccupation diminishes, they have the freshness of mind to deal more effectively with the personal problems that life invariably presents.

Lord, may I come to see today that I'm surrounded by people whose needs are far greater than my own. I want to avoid the inner stagnancy that comes from my lack of concern for others. May I come to know a freshness of spirit that grows from the giving of myself.

Looking Good

If you look at God primarily as a judge, it becomes important to look good before God. You would want to live without mistakes, because your security would be in your own goodness, rather than in God's love. You would be earning your salvation by looking good before God. And if you happened to make a mistake, you would have to repress it, for every mistake would simply arouse the God who would be waiting to judge you.

People who love God and understand his mercy would still want to look good before him, but for reasons quite different from those of people who see God as a judge. The former do good things as a response to the unconditional love of God. The latter do good things in order to earn the acceptance of a judging God.

God loves you unconditionally, and it is his love for you that makes you capable of responding to him. It is never the other way around. God's love is what finally saves you, and it is his love working within you that enables you to look good before him.

I want to stop trying to earn your love, Jesus. That never works, because your love is already unconditionally within me. I simply want to conform my life to that fact, to respond to your free gift of yourself. And I want to believe more deeply that you love me even in the times when I fail.

Reincarnation

Sometimes you hear of people who would like to return to earth after death, perhaps to continue where they left off, or perhaps to live another life. Their wish may come from the hope that they might do things better with another chance. There would be the hope that finally, they might "get it right." But even if it were possible to reincarnate many times, it might never be possible to "get it right." We leave this world with a part of us that is not fully polished. The ultimate polishing takes place as we definitively make a choice for God, but that happens only at the last moment of temporal life, when time and space will never again be able to distract us.

Perhaps the desire to return to earth sometimes comes from a lack of trust in the new life promised to us through the resurrection. The supposition might be that something will be missing and that total fulfillment will elude us. Could this possibly be a denial of the glory and total joy of the resurrection that Jesus invites us to share with him?

Lord, I appreciate this life. It is a gift from you. But, when the time comes, may I be ready to die to it that I might be reborn into the fullness of what you have promised through the resurrection.

Followers

Bear cubs follow the mother bear wherever she leads because they know her as their protector and their source of life. Cubs that would not follow the mother bear would be a strange sight, an anomaly of nature that would not make sense. Perhaps bears are yet another of nature's examples that has something to say to us about ourselves.

If people know Jesus as the source of their lives, then as Jesus' Spirit moves within them, they follow the movement wherever it leads. If followers of Jesus turned away from the motion of his Spirit, they would be anomalies that would make no sense. They come to know the movement of the Spirit by watching the way their day unfolds. Attentive persons know how to be conscious of God's gift of beauty wherever it occurs during the day, for they respond to the Spirit who leads them to notice it. Attentive people know when to relax with God and when to be active in serving the needs of others. They know, because they follow the motion of the Spirit as the Spirit moves within them and within the circumstances of each day. They follow, for they know that the Spirit is the source of their lives.

Lord, may I experience more deeply that your Spirit is the source of my life. May I be attentive to the leading of your Spirit.

Detachment

It seems easier to offer solutions for other people's problems than it is to find solutions for your own, because you can usually be more detached from the problems of others. Guilt, fear, or anger often stand in the way when you try to deal with yourself. But how can you become detached from your own emotions? And if you are not detached, how can you find the requisite clarity to deal with yourself?

The next time you are rocked by any emotion, stand outside of yourself and quietly observe what is going on within you. When you simply look at yourself as an observer, you discover that your emotions are not really you. And since they are separate from you, you have some control over them. This is quite different from suppressing unwanted emotions. You admit that the emotions are there, but you realize that they are not a part of your deepest self. For a moment, you allow yourself to stand away from them and look at them the way you might look at a film or a play.

The more you know how to detach yourself from your emotions, the more you can calmly lessen their influence. Being more calm and detached, you can look at yourself with greater objectivity. You become freer to deal with the personal problems that need to be faced.

I thank you for the gift of my emotions, Lord, but I need to avoid the temptation to be overwhelmed by them. When they threaten to

overwhelm me, may I learn how to quietly de-
tach myself from them.

SEPTEMBER 7

Mixed Strains

A mixed strain in nature is neither this nor that. It is a complex of at least several different things. In the material world of biology and botany, mixed strains often make the best kinds of animals and plants. But in the moral world of human beings, mixed strains often cause the worst kind of human behavior.

Many of us are mixtures, hybrids of honesty and dishonesty, of fidelity and infidelity, of empathy and apathy. We care for others in one moment and neglect them in the next. Our love is a mixed variety, not pure, but tainted by many contrary attitudes. Does this negatively influence our effectiveness in life and cause tepidity of love?

"I know what you have done; I know you are neither cold nor hot. How I wish you were either one or the other! But because you are lukewarm, neither hot nor cold, I am going to spit you out of my mouth" (Rv 3:15–16).

Much of my moral life is a mixture of hot and
cold, a lukewarmness, Lord. I offer you my
heart, that your touch may heal its divisions
and make it pure.

SEPTEMBER 8

Expectancy

After God made his promise to Abraham, Abraham waited patiently for its fulfillment. Abraham's willingness to wait revealed the importance of the promise. In our own lives, we realize the necessity to wait for what is important to us.

For that reason, we wait for God. The waiting says that God is important to us, that we could not do without him. Perhaps God allows us to wait in order to increase our desire for his presence, to deepen our awareness of his importance. In any case, we learn through waiting that we cannot manipulate God. We do not control our relationship with God. God is in control. Waiting teaches us to let go and simply to be attentive. In our expectant attentiveness, we discover our poverty which enables us to be filled with the presence of God.

Lord, sometimes you seem so far away. If I can find nothing in myself that causes the distance, I will simply wait expectantly for the moment when you come to reassure me of your presence. I will wait for you, because you are the meaning of my life.

SEPTEMBER 9

In Step

To be able to pray, we have to be in step with God. When our lives are out of harmony with what we say to God in prayer, prayer soon becomes impossible. How can we be peacefully attentive to God when we are out of step with what God asks us to be?

Fruitful prayer always begins with honesty. We need to ask ourselves if we really want God's will to be done, if we really want to conform ourselves to his wisdom and love in our daily life. If we are out of step with God, our prayer can never be what true prayer is meant to be — an act of adoration that includes the submission of our total being to God. Without being in step with God, we are unable to know the divine friendship that the experience of prayer is meant to give us. Without being in step with God, we cannot know who God is.

Lord, may I end all of my days knowing that I have walked through them in step with you. Pardon the fear that is sometimes still within me whenever I try to let go of doing my own will.

SEPTEMBER 10

Healing Ourselves Through Forgiveness

Then Peter came to Jesus and asked, "Lord, if my brother keeps on sinning against me, how many times do I have to forgive him? Seven times?" "No, not seven times," answered Jesus, "but seventy times seven."

— Matthew 18:21–22

Forgiving someone heals not only the one forgiven, but the forgiver as well. Have you experienced this in your own acts of forgiveness?

When someone hurts us, the hurt stays in our memories, remaining as an irritant long after the hurt was originally experienced. To the extent that we nourish the hurt, we give it the power to poison our lives, to affect our health, and to compromise our peace of mind.

The problem is that we cannot live in this world without experiencing hurt. Even in spite of our best intentions, we hurt one another, and we do not always have the best intentions! So how can we mitigate the pain that comes from the wounds and betrayals inflicted on us by others? There seems to be only one answer — in the act of forgiving. It is in forgiving that painful memories die and we begin to heal ourselves. Forgiving someone who has hurt us becomes an act of gentleness and kindness to ourselves. We become free of the hurt when we forgive the one who caused it. This seems to run counter to worldly wisdom, but forgiveness stems from the wisdom of God. Only one who forgives comes to understand that it is a wisdom that heals.

Lord, may I not cause needless suffering to myself and to others by my refusal to forgive.

SEPTEMBER 11

Call Home

Peace of mind! Is there anyone who does not long for it? Peace of mind is one of the greatest gifts we can enjoy, and yet it can so easily slip away from us.

What threatens your peace of mind? Can you anticipate ways during the day in which it might be lost? And when it threatens to slip away from you, what can you do about it?

Why not try calling home? "Calling home" would be an act of turning our minds to God in trust for the peace that we need to deal with the moment. It would be a moment of quiet when we remove ourselves from what disturbs us, so that we might get the strength and the perspective to cope. God is not indifferent to our problems, but how can we receive his healing presence when we are agitated? In the calmness of our hearts God can come and give the peace that enables us to continue with our lives. And that is what God wants to do. When we call home, we allow ourselves to become aware of his calming presence and to accept his healing strength.

In the midst of my troubles, Lord, may I remember to call home.

SEPTEMBER 12

Slippery Slopes

The Bible tells us that Judas was a thief. How did this dishonesty begin? Perhaps with thoughts about stealing from the common purse? Did it then escalate into petty thievery? We know how it ended — the betrayal of Jesus for thirty pieces of silver. Isn't this sometimes the pattern? We start out with small imperfections, and if we are not careful, we find ourselves on a slippery slope that leads to serious evil. What is the remedy for this?

Examine yourself frequently and be honest. Acknowledge your imperfections. Are they putting you on a slippery slope? Sometimes you discover that they are, but at the moment, the slipping may not seem serious to you. It is so easy to rationalize, but a good remedy for that is to entrust your self-examinations to a respected friend or a spiritual guide. He or she may see more clearly than you. And if you are honest, a caring guide may help you to avoid the tragedy that lies waiting at the bottom for those who play on slippery slopes.

Lord, I ask for the strength to live honestly. Help me to avoid the slippery slopes that I sometimes fail to see.

S E P T E M B E R 13

Choose Life!

"I am now giving you the choice between life and death, between God's blessing and God's curse, and I call heaven and earth to witness the choice you make. Choose life."

— Deuteronomy 30:19

What was promised in the Old Testament has come to fruition in Jesus. We rise to new life with Jesus whenever we die to ourselves and choose a life of love. When we do this, we know the power of the resurrection even in this life. But this is only the beginning. For the life we have now will be transformed and raised up into a life that is eternal. This is the gift of God given to us through Jesus Christ. We do not have to earn it. It is already given. We only have to choose the gift.

This day, Lord, I want to choose whatever is life-giving, no matter what the cost to myself. I want to be mindful of your promises and keep your word so that I might continue to grow toward the fullness of life with you.

SEPTEMBER 14

Guilt

Nothing harms us more than the repression of guilt. Repression siphons off our energy and focuses it on the futile task of trying to hide our feelings. If we repress guilt, we show that we do not feel ourselves to be fully accepted by God. When we come to believe that God's acceptance of ourselves is without limits, then we finally gain the freedom to admit our wrongdoing and accept the gift of reconciliation that is always available to us.

God loves us whether we admit our guilt or not. But without the full trust that includes revealing all that we are, we never come to understand that we are unconditionally loved. This is why the repression of guilt is so harmful. Instead of experiencing ourselves to be one with the God who loves us unconditionally, we choose to be alienated and alone. The choice is senseless, because the peace of God's unconditional love is ours whenever we wish to accept it. This is Jesus' revelation to us, the

Good News that he came to give. How often it is misunderstood.

In the midst of my sinfulness, may I never be afraid of you, Lord. May I never hide from you, for that would be a denial of your unconditional love.

Dreams

Most dreams can only be realized by journeying toward them one step at a time. We have to make the beginning step and travel patiently toward our dreams, satisfied with the progress each day brings. Living one day at a time, we slowly take possession of those dreams that are possible for us to attain.

Pick one of your dreams and ask yourself what step you will take today toward its realization. And then with attention and courage, take the step. In reaching for your attainable dreams, you utilize the potentials placed within you by God. One step at a time, you fashion your life to bring to perfection the gifts God has given you.

Lord, I want to live this day in such a way that I will come closer to the realization of my dreams. May the dreams I choose be in harmony with your will for me.

Freedom

It was late that Sunday evening, and the disciples were gathered together behind locked doors, because they were afraid of the Jewish authorities. Then Jesus came and stood among them. "Peace be with you," he said.

— John 20:19

The disciples were constricted by their fear, confined to a sort of jail of their own making. Their experience can happen to any one of us. Excessive emotions of any kind can constrict us and put us into a psychological straight jacket. Any excessive emotion erodes our ability to be conscious of what is real. We are sometimes in a psychological jail of our own making, and we do not realize it.

The possibility of freedom dawns with the realization that we have enslaved ourselves through an overuse of our emotions. We become free to the extent that we act against the enslavement. The disciples became free when, with the help of Jesus, they effectively realized that they could break through their jail of fear. What enslavement do we have to break before we can call ourselves free?

Lord, give me the courage to break the bonds of those attitudes and emotions that enslave me and rob me of being free. As I have been responsible for my enslavement, so now I will be responsible for my freedom.

A Different Kind of Peace

"Peace is what I leave with you; it is my own peace that I give you. I do not give it as the world does. Do not be worried and upset; do not be afraid."

— John 14:27

How does Jesus' peace differ from the peace offered by the world? Actually, the world cannot offer true peace. It merely offers a temporary fulfillment of desire. It offers material things that satisfy for a time, and then leave us empty again. It offers attitudes about life that may seem to satisfy for a time, but which sell us short later on.

The peace that Jesus gives is a peace that lasts beyond changing external circumstances. It can even coexist with pain and deprivation. For the peace of Jesus is his own presence within ourselves, a presence that brings us the joy of knowing that we belong to the God who alone satisfies our longings. Since his presence is beyond space and time, so is the peace. Those who choose the free gift of Jesus' peace know what this means. The experience of it is beyond words.

Jesus, may I come to know more deeply the peace that you give. The more that I long for it, the more I will be capable of receiving it. Increase my longing.

Justice

"My commandment is this: love one another, just as I love you."

— John 15:12

We receive the command to love one another from Jesus, but there can be no love without justice. When we are unjust to others, we become unloving, and then we are unable to know God who is love.

Justice means sharing our resources with those who are in need. Justice means sharing our time and energy with those who have a right to them. It means giving time to our families, and it means an appropriate giving of our energies to those who pay for our work. Justice means not destroying the life God has created on this planet and not squandering its resources so that our children may have the joy of sharing in them. Justice always gives what is due, and so it is always a mark of love.

When we reflect more deeply on our own life circumstances, our sense of justice is able to expand, and we become more aware of what is required of us. To the extent that we are sensitive to those requirements, our lives are open to love.

Lord, sometimes I forget that there can be no love without justice. Help me to see more clearly the connection between the two.

Mending the Rift

"If your brother sins, rebuke him, and if he repents, forgive him. If he sins against you seven times in one day, and each time he comes to you saying, 'I repent,' you must forgive him."

— Luke 17:3–4

What should be done when a person who hurts another does not ask for forgiveness? Sometimes the person who has been hurt must take the first step in mending the rift. It may be the only way the rift can be healed.

Do what you can to facilitate reconciliation, even though you may not be the one who caused the hurt. In doing this, you are simply doing what God always does, for God always takes the initiative in reconciliation, and his loving forgiveness shines continually on all of us. You become the chief beneficiary of your own kindness, for in doing what God does, you begin to experience the peace that only he can give.

It's hard enough, Lord, to forgive those who ask for it, but to offer it to those who do not ask, that requires a strength beyond mine. And so, Lord, I won't rely on my strength, but rather on yours, and in doing this, my heart will find your peace.

Loving Yourself

Loving yourself means wanting to be the person God created you to be, and doing those things that God wants you to do. It means desiring to attain the attitudes that will make you mature, and bringing to fruition the potentials that God has placed within you.

Anyone living in this way forms himself according to the mind of God who desires all people to grow into the fullness he plans for them. If this is what love of self means, then it seems clear what the love of neighbor should mean. Loving one's neighbor would entail helping someone to grow into the fullness that God has planned for him. Both the love of self and the love of neighbor would have a similar meaning, and with its realization, people would come to experience the joy of a caring human community.

Lord, may I achieve a clearer understanding of a Christian love of self, and may I apply that understanding to the way I love others.

Renewal

Our experiences flow through cycles of light and darkness, a series of ebbs and flows that make up the movement of life. When our creative energies dry up, we begin to wonder if we can ever produce again. When a friendship reaches ebb tide, we wonder if it can be revitalized. In the midst of darkness, we wonder if there will ever be light.

We forget that our lives go in cycles, and that in our past, patterns of darkness or stagnation yielded to surges of new life. Understanding the vital law of ebb and flow, can we have courage during the times of darkness to believe that they are preludes to light and renewal?

I've sometimes forgotten that darkness gives birth to renewal, Lord, and I've allowed myself to become discouraged. To the extent that it's in my power, I will shorten the dark periods of my life by believing in the possibility of light. May I learn how to foster renewal in my life.

SEPTEMBER 22

Stability

In the midst of constant change, people look for a point of stability, a place to stand where they can feel secure. In the external world, we have little experience of stability. The economy changes, our youth slowly changes into age, societal customs and attitudes change. Where is the still point from which we can experience our lives with a sense of certainty?

To find the still point that offers stability, go into the inner core of yourself. The way to your inner core is through meditation. Although an experienced guide may help you to understand and experience something of meditation's fruits, no one can explain to you what you will find as you meditate. One can only invite you to the experience. The experience reveals to you the inner core of your life which is united with God, a core which remains stable beneath all the changes of your life. It is the place where you experience stability and peace in the midst of turbulence and change.

I want to find this stable core within myself, Lord, that I might experience the peace that underlies all the changing aspects of my life. I commit myself to learn more about meditation, and to be faithful in doing it, that I might know the stability it brings.

SEPTEMBER 23

Being There

It would be a tragedy to go through life and never fully experience anything you do. Some people live half-consciously without thinking much about what they do, or without feeling deeply about the events of their lives. Whenever something happens to them, they seem to be somewhere else.

Many of us live with an abstraction, preoccupying ourselves with a past or a future that does not exist. What exists concretely is simply this present moment. Zen philosophy gives us this advice, "When you sit, sit. When you stand, stand. When you eat, eat." In other words, whatever you do, be there. Otherwise, how can you be conscious of your life?

You can be met in each moment of the day, Lord. I don't want to miss any of those moments. I want the joy of fully being there in each one of them.

SEPTEMBER 24

No Escape

It is a common mistake to suppose that new friends, a new joy, or a new place to live will cure whatever inner conflicts we have. There is no escape from inner conflicts. Their pain increases when they are ignored. They can only be healed when they are faced.

To avoid facing inner conflicts is to miss the message they give us. If we know how to read their meaning, our inner conflicts become stimuli for new consciousness and growth. They teach us that we cannot remain as we are and that only in expanding our ways of experiencing and looking at life can we become whole. In this sense, inner conflicts can be valuable allies, but only when they are faced and their messages deciphered.

Lord, you allow inner conflicts as spurs to growth. May I not try to escape from them, but instead may I face them and learn their message.

Suffering

There is a difference between pain and suffering. Pain is a discomfort that we experience in the present moment. Suffering strikes when we not only experience pain, but when we project into the future, wondering how we are going to get through the day, the month, or the year. And suffering strikes even harder when we do not accept pain. But should we accept pain?

Our first response to pain should be to see how we can rid ourselves of it. When it becomes clear that we cannot, then we have no reasonable course other than to accept what cannot be changed. When we fail to do that, pain changes into suffering, and we make the inevitable pains of life worse than they need to be.

Lord, may I not make the burdens of life heavier than they already are.

Worthiness

Is it possible to feel ourselves worthy and unworthy at the same time? From the point of view of God's unconditional love, we are always worthy. God declares us worthy by the fact that he continually gives us his unconditional love. From a human point of view, we may experience ourselves as unworthy, because we do not accept God's love or live in harmony with what God asks of us. We can block ourselves off from God's love by not receiving it, but we can never stop God from giving it.

Worthiness is one of the paradoxes of life. Our own lack of worthiness can exist only from our point of view, not God's. God may look upon us and see that we do not accept the love he offers, but his unconditional love continues regardless of that. And yet, he will never force us to accept his love. It seems like something of a puzzle, but that is only because we have difficulty taking God at his word. God's love never fluctuates, but ours does. That is where we have the problem.

I choose to believe in your unconditional love, Lord, and I thank you that you shower me with it even in those times when I shut myself off from you. You are the one who makes me worthy, for without your unconditional love, I would be nothing at all.

SEPTEMBER 27

The Whisper

"Go out and stand before me on top of the mountain," the Lord said to him. Then the Lord passed by and sent a furious wind that split the hills and shattered the rocks — but the Lord was not in the wind. The wind stopped blowing, and then there was an earthquake — but the Lord was not in the earthquake. After the earthquake there was a fire — but the Lord was not in the fire.

And after the fire there was the soft whisper of a voice.

When Elijah heard it, he covered his face with his cloak and went out and stood at the entrance of the cave. A voice said to him, "Elijah, what are you doing here?"

— 1 Kings 19:11–13

The Lord's presence was not in the wind, not in the earthquake, nor in the fire, but only in the soft whispering voice. God reveals his presence in quiet and stillness. Unless we know how to be still, we will miss him. Is it any different in our relationships with human beings? We have to be quietly attentive to them, or else our own inner noise drowns out our ability to hear them.

We will have difficulty knowing God's presence in our daily activities if we never learn to listen quietly, and to find him in the still moments of our lives.

Lord, teach me to be quiet so that the noise within me may be silenced. In the stillness may I become aware of your presence.

SEPTEMBER 28

Commitment

God is a God who involves himself in human history. The epitome of his involvement took place at the time of the incarnation of his Son. Although God always cared for the world, the incarnation of his Son was a concrete sign to us that he was committed to what he had made. His commitment to us continues through his presence in each of us. We know his commitment to us through his Spirit which fills us with love and guides us to respond to the needs of others.

God invites us to share in his commitment to the world. If we say we love others, then we must incarnate that love among them, as God has incarnated his love among us. In doing that, we demonstrate that our commitment is real.

Lord, as you have given yourself to me, so I give myself to you and to my brothers and sisters. May I be committed in act and not just in thought, so that my commitment might be real.

SEPTEMBER 29

Don't Send Me, Lord

The Lord said to me, "I chose you before I gave you life, and before you were born I selected you to be a prophet to the nations." I answered, "Sovereign Lord, I don't know how to speak; I am too young." But the Lord said to me, "Do not say that you are too young, but go to the people I send you to, and tell them everything I command you to say. Do not be afraid of them, for I will be with you to protect you. I, the Lord, have spoken!"

— Jeremiah 1:4–8

The Lord sends Jeremiah, and Jeremiah is unable to offer an acceptable excuse as to why he should not go. All his excuses are invalidated by the Lord's promise to be with him in his task. Nothing more needs to be said.

From Jeremiah, we learn a valuable lesson. We are asked to forget our inadequacies as we hear God's invitation to work in his world. It is his power that gives us the courage and ability to do what he wants from us. Our woundedness, our fear, our selfishness, our anxieties — God is capable of overcoming all of these by the power of his presence. When God calls us to a task, there is no excuse for not responding to his call.

Lord, you know my inadequacies, and yet you still call me to serve those who are a part of my life. May I trust in the power of your presence which enables me to do your will.

SEPTEMBER 30

Reasons

Why do we do the things we do? Do we serve God in order to win his approval, or do we serve him in order to respond to his love? Do we love our friends simply because we are attracted to them, or do we love them because of who they are? Are we kind and generous toward others in order to gain respect, or are we kind and generous because we want to serve? Sometimes we do the right things for the wrong reasons, and so it is important for us to ask ourselves why we do the things we do.

Doing the right things for the wrong reasons erodes the goodness of what we do. It even erodes the success of our actions, for things done out of selfishness are done without the insight and care that make them fully efficacious. The most successful persons in life are those who act with the greatest amount of selflessness. They have the insight to give to others what they most need to receive.

Lord, may I have the insight to understand the reasons for what I do. May I be able to convert what is selfish in me to an attitude of love, so that I might more effectively care for others.

OCTOBER

OCTOBER 1

Five Loaves and Two Fish

He ordered the people to sit down on the grass; then he took the five loaves and the two fish, looked up to heaven, and gave thanks to God. He broke the loaves and gave them to the disciples, and the disciples gave them to the people. Everyone ate and had enough. Then the disciples took up twelve baskets full of what was left over. The number of men who ate was about five thousand, not counting the women and children.

— Matthew 14:19–21

Dinner for several thousand from five loaves and two fish? Did this miracle happen only once in history, or is it possible for it to happen over and over again?

With only one thousand dollars, a recovering alcoholic in a midwestern city rented and renovated a club building for alcoholics. Within five years, the club was able to purchase not only the building, but two half-way houses besides. With the equivalent of five loaves and two fish, plus some courage and imagination, one man made a difference to many poor alcoholics in his city.

The gospel often challenges us to ask ourselves what we do for the needy. Our hands are empty before the Lord if we have no answer to the question. What possibilities do we have of sharing our resources, even if they are as meager as those used by Jesus? What possibilities do we have of sharing our time and energies with those who need them, even when those energies are in short supply? Acts of kindness that we do for others may seem quite small to us, but they often multiply into huge benefits in the lives of those who receive them. That is the lesson of the loaves and fish.

Jesus, you did so much with so little. May I have the love and imagination to imitate you.

OCTOBER 2

The Hurt Child

Deep inside most of us is a child whose hurts have never been fully healed. This is a basic problem for many in life. Childhood disappointments, misunderstandings, sadness, and fears have been buried and forgotten under the layers of passing years. Sometimes these hurts make their presence felt in later life by a sense of uneasiness that we do not know how to explain.

Forgiveness of those who hurt us in our childhood begins to heal the hurt child within ourselves. Acceptance and love of our hurt child carries the healing a step further.

Acknowledge the hurt child within yourself and take care of it. This requires some healthy self-introspection, and it is sometimes a painful process. It is, however, the only way to healing. If you remain unconscious of your hurt child and do not accept and love it, then the child continues to disturb you. When you acknowledge it with love and understanding, then you integrate the child into your personality, and it becomes a source of wholeness.

I realize, Lord, that the hurt child is a part of me. With courage I want to acknowledge and love it, and to forgive those who have caused my childhood hurts so that I might be free and whole.

OCTOBER 3

Moment by Moment

The choices of each moment are the building blocks that form us to be who we are. The moments of each day present us with options — the option to respond to someone's needs or to ignore them; the option to trust in God or to trust only in ourselves; the option to indulge in a harmful habit or to liberate ourselves and be free. For the awake person, many moments each day bring the possibilities of choice and growth. The way we live those moments determines the tenor of our lives.

When we look at the way we live our daily moments, we come to see what we have made ourselves to be. What do you discover about yourself from the way you use the moments of your day?

I need a greater appreciation for the meaning of the individual moments of my life, Lord. May I not waste the gifts of growth they bring.

OCTOBER 4

Being Alive

For most of us, the sense of being fully alive does not come automatically. We gradually learn to do the things that cause us to feel alive. The learning experience is different for all of us. We have to discover for ourselves what it is that causes the sense of aliveness. We have to be willing to experiment.

Sometimes long habits of unconsciousness block out your memories of what caused you to feel alive in the past. Reflect on your past. What were the experiences in your life that caused you to feel most joyful and most awake? It also helps to experiment with new experiences in the present. This requires some imagination and a willingness to try something different, perhaps even to do things you have never tried before.

Being alive would include paying attention to what the present moment is actually offering to us. That alone would bring a richness to the present that we often miss. Much of our lives passes us by without affecting us because often we are only half awake.

We can deepen the sense of being alive, but only if we pay some attention to what we are feeling at the present moment, recapture what was good from the past, and broaden our vision as to what is possible in the future.

Lord, I thank you for the gift of life. May I deepen my experience of the gift you have given.

O C T O B E R 5

It's Just the Way I Am

What a great way to avoid responsibility for who we are and what we do. We need only say to ourselves or to others, "It's just the way I am." The phrase implies that we have no control over who we are and what we do. What we think, feel, and do can then be blamed on the influence of others, or on forces beyond our control. If we fail, if we are angry or depressed, someone else is responsible for it.

It is true, of course, that we have all suffered some negative influences from others, and that adverse circumstances at times have touched each of us. But a core of freedom remains within us, and it is there, at the core of our being, where we have relative freedom to shape our lives. Relative freedom is quite enough for responsible decisions, and in this life, relative freedom is all we are ever going to have.

The honest person takes responsibility for his or her life without excuses, for personal responsibility is the truth of life. Without this truth, there can be no human community.

Lord, I thank you for my freedom. Give me the honesty and courage to accept the responsibility that freedom demands.

OCTOBER 6

A Time to Make Peace

There is a time to make peace, a time to reconcile ourselves to the Father for refusing to become the persons he created us to be.

There is a time to make peace, a time to reconcile ourselves to the Son for refusing to listen attentively to the word which is his gift to us.

There is a time to make peace, a time to reconcile ourselves to the Holy Spirit for refusing the inspirations spoken quietly to us in the depth of our hearts.

There is a time to make peace, a time to reconcile ourselves to our brothers and sisters for ignoring their needs.

If we discover a lack of peace in our lives, let us ask if it is not time for reconciliation, as well as a time for us to forgive ourselves.

Lord, while there is still time, show me where I need to make peace and give me the courage to make it.

Fellow Travelers

Suffering seems worse when we think we suffer alone. A feeling of isolation touches us when we imagine that others are immune from the kinds of disappointments and failures that we often have. But the truth is that all of us are in the same stream of life, sharing in the experience of similar disappointments and failures.

We often forget that we are all fellow-travelers in life, and that none of us is a stranger to life's pains and disappointments. No matter how unusual or embarrassing our own predicaments may seem, someone else has experienced them before us. With millions of people on this earth, how could anything we experience be entirely unique? Much comfort can be found in this truth. Knowing that we are a part of the stream of life with all of its struggles and failures, we know that we are not alone, that our failures do not mark us as odd or unique. They simply signify that we are human. We struggle along with all of our brothers and sisters to pull ourselves up and move along as best we can.

Lord, I know that you are with me in my predicaments and failures, but I need to know that these sufferings are not unique to my life. May I have the insight to understand that all my brothers and sisters struggle with similar sufferings in their lives. May this insight help me to grow in compassion for myself and for others.

OCTOBER 8

Friendship

Friendships are one of the major joys of life. It is important to do those things that preserve them and foster their growth. If we have developed a friendship, the implication is that we have committed ourselves to remain faithful to it. The expectation is that our friend will also be committed to faithfulness. When fidelity is violated, there is need for an honest talk.

Honesty is the bedrock of friendship. Sometimes we need to confront a friend in various ways for his own good in order to help him grow, and the honesty can be painful. Caring confrontation should always take into account another person's feelings. Care for another person's feelings as you would care for your own.

Be grateful for your friends. Let them know you appreciate them, for they are gifts that deeply enrich your life.

Thank you, Lord, for your friendship, and for all the friends in my life. They mirror your love for me. May I be faithful to them.

OCTOBER 9

Blunders

You can regard a blunder negatively, simply looking at it as an unredeemable failure. You can also take a blunder and learn something from it. In that case, a blunder becomes an opportunity for growth.

Unfortunately, you cannot completely avoid making blunders, but you can change the way you look at them. If you simply brood over your mistakes, you learn nothing from them. If they do not become learning experiences, you may be condemned to repeat them. It takes some quiet introspection to see what can be learned from a blunder. For those who learn, even their *faux pas* can contribute to their happiness and growth.

I usually get disgusted with myself, Lord, when I look at my mistakes. I guess this amounts to a lot of wasted energy and a false sense of pride. May I learn to profit from my blunders instead of being angry with myself for committing them.

O C T O B E R 10

Bending

Trees have the ability to sway in the wind, to bend with the power of a storm. If they were unable to bend, their chances of survival in the midst of gales and storms would be far less. It is the same with us. We need to bend in order for ourselves and others to survive peacefully.

Bending in this sense would have nothing to do with compromising about basic principles. Instead, it would be open to compromise in those areas where inviolable values would not be violated and where no harm would be done to others. Bending would include the willingness to look at other points of view, to avoid the storms of stubbornness that keep people from accommodating themselves to others.

Bending in this sense is akin to love. It looks to the good of others rather than to one's own. An appropriate willingness to bend creates part of the charm of a loving family and community life, and it is one of the ingredients in the cement that holds friendships together.

Lord, grant me an understanding heart and suppleness of mind and spirit, so that I might relate more caringly to others.

OCTOBER 11

If Only I Had Known

When I was young, I could never understand why our family car was so old. When it finally wore out, I could not understand why its replacement was another bottom-of-the-line model. I did not understand until I graduated from high school. At that point, my dad told me that he had saved a fairly considerable sum for my college education. That revelation explained a lot of things. If only I had known.

We often have misconceptions about why people do what they do, or why they are the way they are. This is especially true when we are continually irritated by the behavior of others. We forget that a grouchy person may be ill; or that an aloof person may never have been loved; or that a frightened person may never have known the security of an accepting family. We see behavior in others that we cannot understand because we do not know the reasons behind it. We cannot judge, but we can give love, and if there is a need for change in ourselves or in others, the love we give may be the catalyst for it.

Lord, give me the gift of understanding, and help me to avoid judging others.

OCTOBER 12

Humility

The attitude you should have is the one that Christ Jesus had: He always had the nature of God, but he did not think that by force he should try to become equal with God. Instead of this, of his own free will he gave up all he had, and took the nature of a servant. He became like man and appeared in human likeness.

— Philippians 2:5–7

What are we to make of the outward appearance Jesus presents to us — the Son of God serving others and even hanging on a cross? Arms outstretched, his whole body lifeless, what kind of message was Jesus giving to those who saw him?

Jesus could have come down from the cross in a blaze of glory. He might have been accepted immediately, had he put on a dazzling display, but would he have been loved? To prove his love and win ours, he made a decision to hang, broken and seemingly helpless, on a cross.

One of the lessons of the cross is that caring, humble service is more loveable than power, force, and arrogance. Winning the cooperation of others is one of the powerful results of humble, caring service. Perhaps we accomplish more by serving gently and humbly than we do by using coercion and arrogance.

Lord, may my service to my brothers and sisters be humble and caring. When it is necessary for me to be assertive, may I do so with kindness.

OCTOBER 13

Enemies

"You have heard that it was said, 'Love your friends, hate your enemies.' But now I tell you: love your enemies and pray for those who persecute you, so that you may become the sons of your Father in heaven. For he makes his sun to shine on bad and good people alike, and gives rain to those who do good and to those who do evil."

— Matthew 5:43–45

Love your enemy. If you do, it makes life easier for you. Can you imagine how much energy is lost when you hate or resent someone? How many of us have that much energy to spare?

If there is someone in your life who is difficult to love, commend that person to God. If that person needs your help, ask God for the strength to give it.

Of course, no one said that this would be easy. Loving those who are difficult to love goes against the grain of our egos. But we are not required to have warm feelings for them. We are simply required to pray for their good, and if the occasion arises, to do good to them. From all of this, our enemies receive our forgiveness, and from our act of forgiveness, we receive peace of mind and the joy of knowing that we live according to God's will.

Lord, I wish to regard no person as my enemy, but I know that it takes great humility to love those who don't love me. Grant me the strength to do what you ask of me.

OCTOBER 14

Passion for Life

Passion for life seems to come more naturally to some than it does to others. We have to allow ourselves to be amazed by life every day, or else the passion within us slowly dies.

Today, allow yourself to be amazed at God's tremendous unconditional love for you. Reflect on his gift of creation, his death and resurrection for you, and re-kindle your passion for God.

Today, allow yourself to be amazed at the love you have received from others. Reflect on these gifts of love and re-kindle your passion for life.

Today, allow yourself to see more clearly, to hear more intently, to touch more consciously. Reflect on these experiences of awareness and re-kindle your passion for consciousness.

Know the gifts you have received. In appreciating them more fully, your passion for life will deepen.

Lord, may I not be half asleep in the midst of the abundance within and around me. Rekindle within me a desire to live fully. Rekindle within me a passion for life.

O C T O B E R 15

The Importance of You

God created you with care, making sure that you would always be one of a kind, always unique in this world. God also lived, died, and rose for you, and in doing these things, he revealed to you a beautiful truth: you are important to God. At every moment of your life, you are in the mind of God. God cannot forget about you, for he can never forget what he has made. Again, the message comes clearly: you are important to God.

If we believe all of this to be true, why do we so often undervalue ourselves? Has the meaning of God's love for us really reached our hearts? When we fully understand the message, our past failures no longer matter so much. In spite of our weaknesses and lack of love, we always remain important to God. This is what the gospel tells us. No wonder the word gospel means "good news."

I have a difficult time believing that I am important to you, Lord, and yet, that is what your words and actions reveal to me. All I can do, all you want me to do, is humbly to accept this gift and to say, "Thank you, my God."

O C T O B E R 16

Confidence

Full, loving friendship with God has little to do with being spiritually successful in our own eyes. Instead, it has everything to do with confidence in God's goodness in the midst of our frailties and failures.

What God wants from us is complete trust in him and a joyful acceptance of our human condition. He alone makes this possible for us. Giving complete trust to God is probably the most difficult thing asked of us, but if we say no, nothing else we do will ever substitute for our refusal.

Unwavering confidence in God is the most important gift for which we can ask, because our peace and oneness with God depend upon it. At some point in our lives, we realize this truth, for a time comes when we seem to stand before God powerless and with empty hands. At that moment, we come to know that his accepting love is all that matters. It is our confidence in God that enables us to find our primary meaning in his love rather than in our accomplishments.

Lord, I bring you today all of the confidence of which I am capable. I know this is the gift that you most want to receive from me. May my trust in you remain strong in the midst of my darkness and weakness.

271

Being Patient With Yourself

Pay attention today to the way you treat yourself. If you frequently become impatient with yourself, will you be able to avoid being impatient with others?

Impatience with ourselves may not necessarily stem from a desire to become better because of our love for God. Instead, it often stems from the fact that we allow our faults to bruise our egos. It is the bruised ego that cries out with impatience whenever it catches itself in a mistake.

Impatience with ourselves is just another way in which we foolishly waste a lot of our energy on nothing at all. The more we brood about our human condition, the less energy we have for the constructive activities and projects that add meaning to our lives.

People who are impatient with themselves take themselves too seriously. The next time you make an irritating mistake, try laughter. Wise people know how to laugh at themselves, and in the laughter they learn to accept their mistakes while preserving a sense of self-worth and healthy self-love.

My impatience with myself is just another sign of my untamed egoism, Lord. I see so much evidence of it in my daily life. Instead of being preoccupied with an exaggerated sensitivity to my mistakes, may I learn to pay more attention to the needs of others.

Forgotten Blessings

It is hard to speak about forgotten blessings and to be thankful for them, simply because they are forgotten. And so today, let us take time to remember. Travel back in time and remember the love that touched your childhood. Perhaps much of what you received has been forgotten, its importance dimmed through the passage of time. Remembering brings back a sense of contentment and gratitude. You come to be mindful of how much you have received from others, and how the lives of others who loved you have so beautifully influenced your own.

Perhaps you might also remember those events that you may have tended to regard as lucky breaks, occurrences that opened up spiritual opportunities to you or occurrences that saved you from harm. Can you see in these the presence of God lovingly directing your life?

Remember, too, the blessings that you may consider ordinary, the ones you forget because you take them for granted. Your health and your native talents fit here. Have you sometimes forgotten that these are blessings?

Bringing forgotten blessings back to memory is an act of gratitude to God from whom the blessings flow. In our remembering we are filled with thankfulness and joy.

May I be mindful of the many blessings I have received, Lord. Let my mindfulness change my insensitivity into gratitude, and my cynicism into trust.

Into Your Hands, O Lord

Jesus cried out in a loud voice, "Father! In
your hands I place my Spirit!"

— Luke 23:46

The greatest act of worship we can give God is to
place our lives into his hands. The fullness of the
gift can only be given when time ends for us, when
we are asked to surrender everything in total trust
to God. In the meantime, there are numerous opportunities for surrendering what we can into the
caring hands of God. We let go of childhood in order to grow into adolescence. We let go of adolescence in order to grow into adulthood. Finally, we
gradually surrender the strength of young adulthood as we grow in age. Everything we have is
given back in trust to the source from which it came.

Throughout our lives, we gradually let go of
the goals and pleasures that once served our needs
so that we can grow into the enjoyment of new
ones. This is what it means to grow in wisdom.
We let go of what was once useful to us, because
our changing lives make new demands and present
new opportunities. Ideally, as we grow in wisdom,
we let go of selfish and material goals in order to
embrace altruistic and spiritual ones.

Letting go and surrendering our lives to God
is sometimes painful, but the growth we experience
from the surrender leads to a sense of fulfillment.
Hanging on to what served us in the past prevents

us from becoming the fully developed persons that we were created to be.

Daily, I wish to surrender my life into your hands, Lord, until I make the ultimate surrender that leads to the complete fulfillment of eternal life. May I have the courage to say daily, "Father, in your hands I place my spirit."

OCTOBER 20

Admitting Our Faults

If God already knows our faults, why do we need to admit them? God, of course, needs no extra information from us in order to know what is going on within our hearts. The admission of our faults is more for our sake than for his. We need to be forgiven, but how can we be open to forgiveness if we cannot admit the need?

Healing can only be experienced by those who are able to admit their need for it. What remains hidden and unacknowledged in ourselves cannot be healed. We cheat ourselves by thinking that our wrongdoing can be hidden. It cannot be. The poison of deliberate faults and sins infects us even on an unconscious level, and we come to know its effects through feelings of guilt, unhappiness, and anger toward others. The poisonous effects can only be healed through an admission of guilt which allows God's ever present forgiveness to touch us.

I know there is no easy way out, Lord, and that I can't avoid facing my guilt. It's only through my honest admission of sin that I can be healed and forgiven. Help me to be honest.

OCTOBER 21

Seeing More Clearly

On the occasion of his fiftieth wedding anniversary, a man said to his wife, "When I married you fifty years ago, I thought I could never love you more than I did then. But I was wrong. After fifty years of being with you, I love you more, so much more."

Fifty years of shared life enabled the man to see much more clearly who his wife really was, and to appreciate more deeply all that she meant to him. As his seeing became clearer, his love grew deeper, and he regarded his marriage with an ever growing joy. Here is a standard by which this marriage could be regarded as truly successful.

Perhaps there is a similar standard by which we could judge the tenor of our lives. If we could say about our lives what the man in the story said about his marriage, that would be a sign that our lives have been truly successful. If we love life more in the present than we did in the past, then the man's experience in the story would be our experience as well. If we have gradually grown more conscious of love, of creation, of God, then our appreciation of life will have increased. Having seen the gifts of life more clearly as our years have passed, we will have become more alive. And if we have responded with a more conscious love to what we have seen, our lives will have gradually grown more precious to us through the passage of time.

Lord, sharpen my vision that I may grow in appreciation for your gift of life. May I respond fully to all that it offers as well as to all that it demands.

O C T O B E R 22

Time Off

"Let us go off by ourselves to some place where we will be alone and you can rest a while."

— Mark 6:31

In spite of all that needed to be done, Jesus invited his followers to take time off and rest. When you are too busy to take time off, that may be the time when you need to do it the most. If you plan relaxation as a part of your day, you may lessen those occasions when you are unable to find time for the quiet moments that bring renewal. How can you avoid personal impoverishment if you do not take the time to relax and refresh yourself?

Are you concerned that taking time away from your activities will make you less productive? Perhaps the concern is misplaced. It seems unlikely that any of us can be fully productive without the refreshment of time off. Continual work brings with it the law of diminishing returns. Eventually the returns become meager indeed. Have you ever noticed that in your life?

If you find yourself becoming compulsive about work, if you find yourself growing short-tempered, if you are becoming troublesome to others, think about taking some time off. Somehow the world will manage to get by while you relax, and it will even be better off if you return to it refreshed.

Lord, just as you invited your followers to rest, so you invite me. May I understand the importance of the invitation so that I might avoid the harm that comes from refusing to take time off.

OCTOBER 23

Watching

You can slowly change your life by watching how others live. Would you like to become more patient? Watch a patient person and observe what he or she does. If you like what you see, you can assimilate the behavior into your own life, and slowly learn how to become a patient person. The method of watching works for any of the virtues that you might want to incorporate into your life. You simply have to search for the role models whose virtues you would like to make your own.

The reverse, of course, is also true. You can be influenced by negative role models. But even here, something can be learned. If you are repelled by morally deficient role models, you may be strengthened in choosing the contrasting good.

Above all, watch Jesus as his life unfolds before you in scripture. Paying attention to his values and loving his goodness, you begin to experience that his values gradually become yours. Watching carefully and encountering Jesus in quiet prayer, you find help and encouragement in becoming the person you want to be.

Open my eyes, Lord, that I might watch and learn from you and from others. May my attentive watching reveal to me the goodness in others, and help me in becoming the person you created me to be.

OCTOBER 24

Risks

Much of our growth depends on our willingness to take risks. There is no growth without love, but offering love to others is sometimes a risk. How can you be sure the offering will be received? Deciding to take a new direction in life is sometimes a risk. How can you be sure it will succeed? At certain points of our lives, trusting God may seem like a risk. How can you be sure that he will come through for you? Trusting in people is certainly a risk. How can you be sure you will not be betrayed?

Those who are inordinately afraid of taking risks miss many of the joys of life. They are constrained by fear, and fearful constraint is sometimes a tragedy. The fear of risks keeps people from the discovery of life and the joys of love.

Part of the wisdom of life is to know when to take a risk and when to avoid it. Perhaps only a calm and prayerful mind can ever be that wise. Wisdom comes from God and we have to seek it in confident prayer. Wisdom can also come from our friends, and the insights of a wise friend about risks can be of great help to us.

Where there is no risk, there is no full life. Until we are raised through resurrection to a life beyond space and time, this is the way it will always be. Life is for the courageous, and only the courageous are able to discover the fullness that it offers.

Even you take risks, Lord. Didn't you take one when you made me? Help me to find the middle road between rashness and timidity that I might live with wisdom and courage. Help me not to fear appropriate risks so that I might realize the full potentials of my life.

OCTOBER 25

Who Do You Say I Am?

Jesus went to the territory near the town of Caesarea Philippi, where he asked his disciples, "Who do people say the Son of Man is?" "Some say John the Baptist," they answered. "Others say Elijah, while others say Jeremiah or some other prophet." "What about you?" he asked them. "Who do you say I am?" Simon Peter answered, "You are the Messiah, the Son of the living God."

— Matthew 16:13–16

This is always the question Jesus puts before us, because our answer is never complete. Our understanding of the question grows. When our understanding ceases to grow, we are in trouble. With weak understanding there is weak faith, and a corresponding inability to accept fully the love that Jesus wills to give.

Jesus' own relatives thought that they knew him well enough. "'Isn't he the carpenter's son? Isn't Mary his mother, and aren't James, Joseph, Simon, and Judas his brothers? Aren't all his sisters living here? Where did he get all this?' And so they rejected him" (Mt 13:55–57). Because their vision of Jesus had stopped growing, they had little faith, little openness to the good that Jesus wanted to do for them.

We can never know enough about Jesus. Whatever we think of him, we never have the full picture of who he is. And when his love no longer interests us, then we will have discovered the tragic inadequacy of our understanding.

Lord, may I never think that I fully know who you are. May I listen intently in quiet prayer to your word, that my faith in you might grow, and that my ability to receive your caring help might increase.

O C T O B E R 26

Sharing

"You yourselves know that I have worked with these hands of mine to provide everything that my companions and I have needed. I have shown you in all things that by working hard in this way we must help the weak, remembering the words that the

Lord Jesus himself said, 'There is more happiness in giving than in receiving.' "

— Acts 20:34–35

Whatever gifts we have in our lives are given not just for ourselves, but also for the sake of others. Our personal gifts and talents tend to lose their meaning if they are not in some way shared with others and used for their good. One of our deepest joys is to know that our lives have borne fruit for those whose lives we have been privileged to touch.

Through the sharing of our gifts with others, we discover that major benefits come to ourselves. Sharing with others has a strong effect on our own happiness and sense of fulfillment. It gives meaning to the present and hope for our future, because if we have shared with others, we shall not stand empty-handed before God.

Just as we have received much from others, so we need to share generously from what we have received.

Thank you, Lord, for the richness of the blessings you have given to me, and for all the kindness I have received from others. I am sorry for all those times when I haven't shared my blessings or returned the kindness given to me. Today, I will look for a way to give to others from the gifts that I have received.

The Tax Collector

After this, Jesus went out and saw a tax collector named Levi, sitting in his office. Jesus
said to him, "Follow me." Levi got up, left
everything, and followed him.

— Luke 5:27–28

Levi worked as a tax collector. He was held in low
esteem by the Jews, because he collected taxes from
them for the Romans. But there was another side to
Levi, and Jesus brought this side of his personality
to life when he said, "Follow me."

When we understand that God acknowledges
us through unconditional love, and that he calls
us to follow him and share in his life, we become
alive through the knowledge that we are accepted.
A side of our personalities that laid dormant is re-
awakened. Knowing that we are called and loved,
we discover a courage to let down our barriers and
accept the love of God that makes us whole. When
the truth of God's love for us reaches our hearts,
we are changed.

Something similar happens when we acknowledge one another with love. The care we receive
from others gives us the courage to accept ourselves
and to see ourselves as having value. Believing in
our own value, we have the courage to give love to
others.

Just as love freed Levi to change his life and
to follow the call of God, so love frees us to change
our lives and to follow Jesus wherever he leads us.

Through your call to me, Lord, I find my value and my freedom to risk loving others. Thank you, Lord, for your love that makes me free.

OCTOBER 28

The Call

The twelve apostles were the first to receive and to respond to the direct call of Jesus. As they gathered into the first community of Jesus' disciples, their bond of unity was their hunger for God and their growing belief in Jesus. And yet, as with all human beings, they were plagued with faults.

Peter, though bold at times, could also be fearful and cowardly. The sons of Zebedee were prone to violence. Judas was a traitor. And all of the apostles were slow to catch the meaning of Jesus' death and resurrection. Yet, Jesus worked through these men to establish a community of faith to which we too have been invited.

Each one of us has been called to faith in Jesus, and each of us has received the invitation to spread his message. In our own way, we do what the apostles did, but, like them, we bring our defects with us. Instead of worrying about our defects, we should work with complete confidence in God. In the midst of our defects, God accomplishes his purposes simply because he is God. So long as our trust is in him rather than in ourselves, we will be able to do what he asks of us. His power is greater than our weakness, and his love is strong enough to accomplish within us whatever it wills.

Lord, I hear your call to me. Increase my confidence in you. So long as I trust you to help me, I need not waste time worrying about my defects. I place them in your hands and turn my energies to respond to your call as well as I can.

OCTOBER 29

When God Says, "No"

The person who completely understood God's will would always know how to pray for the right things. But is there anyone who always completely understands God's will? Can we say for sure that it would always be in our best interests if God answered every one of our prayers with a "yes"?

Hindsight probably teaches us to be grateful that some of our prayers were not answered as we had hoped. Sometimes a "no" is the most loving response that God can give. The meaning of this truth often appears somewhat paradoxical to our understanding, but then, how could it be otherwise? The vision of God is too vast for us to grasp. We can only approach God with the faith that believes he will do what is best for us, and sometimes, especially in moments of deep pain, this is a difficult approach indeed. Our understanding is simply left with mystery, and with hope in the promise of God's loving presence even in the midst of our darkness.

Lord, when I suffer deep disappointments, it is sometimes difficult for me to believe in your loving care. Many times I am left in darkness when prayers which seem so legitimate to me are answered with a "no." Help me to develop the attitude that you had when you prayed to your Father. In trust, you said, "Your will be done."

OCTOBER 30

Natural Pleasures

Unfortunately, too many people in our society try to capture euphoria through pills, alcohol, and various forms of other drugs. It never completely works. Those who seek euphoria through drugs find that the experience eventually betrays them. And yet, everyone needs some pleasurable moments in life. We owe it to ourselves to find those pleasures that can bring us good feelings in natural ways. Life offers many such possibilities if we pay attention to them.

If your body feels reasonably well when you get out of bed, the day has already started with a plus. To start your day with awareness of the natural pleasures of life, spend time savoring your coffee and enjoying your breakfast. If the weather is nice, enjoy the sun. If it is raining, enjoy the rain. Perhaps there are some natural pleasures that you can anticipate. Are there at least a few compatible people whom you will see today? Can you look forward to quiet time with a book, music, or favorite television program at the end of the day? Can you look forward to quiet time with your God?

Somewhere within the next twenty-four hours, natural pleasures are waiting for you. They are gifts of God. Will you be aware of them when they come?

Lord, your will is for me to be joyful, to be open to the natural pleasures of life which are your gifts. Thank you for these pleasures. May I be mindful of all that you give.

O C T O B E R 31

Real Presence

"My Father will love him, and my Father and I will come to him and live with him."
— John 14:23

If God is a real presence in our lives, he must be much more than just an idea in our heads. Through prayer and meditation, we grow to sense God's love and to know that he is totally present to us. Through our attentiveness to God, we begin to experience that he is loving us and leading us as we live each day.

God's presence is always real, but our awareness of it comes and goes. Even in our moments of dryness and darkness when our awareness dims, God is totally present to us. The Muslims have a beautiful saying, "God is closer to you than your neck vein."

Though God is always present to us, his presence grows more fruitful to the extent that we become aware of it. The ability to be aware is God's gift. Our task is to be open to the gift through a life receptive to God's presence, a receptivity that grows as we grow in silent expectation.

Lord, I ask for the perseverance to remain attentive to your presence. May I realize more clearly that you are the goal of my life.

NOVEMBER

NOVEMBER 1

The Will of God

"May your will be done on earth as it is in heaven."

— Matthew 6:10

Genuine prayer always asks that God's will be done, not ours. We might prefer it the other way around, but it is our will that often causes us problems. Prayer gets us in touch with the mind of God, and gives us the strength to do his will. This makes sense if we come to see that God's will is finally what is best for us. This, too, we learn in prayer. In silent communication with God, we learn many things that are ultimately for our own benefit. It is through prayer that we learn to accept the things we cannot change, and it is through prayer that we get the strength to change the things we can.

Prayer teaches us to accept life, and through our acceptance of life we learn more deeply how to find God. Prayer does this for us, because it puts us in touch with God, and it is only in the presence of God that we learn to accept life. Acceptance brings wisdom and peace, the peace of God which soothes our lives and gradually enables us to do his will with joy.

It is your will, Lord, that I want to seek. Your will is what is best for me, although I can't understand this until I learn to trust in you. Give me an increase of trust, for without this, I can't live in peace or know the beauty of your presence.

NOVEMBER 2

Advice

It is a hard lesson to learn, but one day we finally come to accept that we cannot handle everything in our lives by ourselves. In moments of darkness and uncertainty, we need someone to walk through the journey of life with us.

Seek out a wise person to walk with you when the light on your path loses its clarity. A wise person will not necessarily tell you what to do, but he or she can point out to you what your options are. Many of us fail to see the number of possibilities open to us when we look for clarity of direction in our lives. Someone else often sees what we cannot.

When we ask advice from someone who is wise, we increase our possibilities of acting successfully in the choices we make. A good advisor will not free us from the responsibility of making our own decisions, but he or she can broaden our vision so that we will have a better chance of making the right ones. If we are sufficiently honest to acknowledge our own limitations, we will have the openness to seek advice in those times when we most need it.

I know that wise advisors are your gifts to me, Lord, and that you sometimes choose to speak to me through them. Help me to break away from the illusion that I don't need them, and grant me the humility to accept wise advice when it is offered.

NOVEMBER 3

Impossibilities

"You must be perfect — just as your Father in heaven is perfect."

— Matthew 5:48

Jesus' words make demands on us that we cannot possibly fulfill by ourselves. They cause us to realize that putting the gospel message into practice is beyond what we are able to do. One possible response to this is to dilute the gospel's meaning, or to whittle it down to our size so that we can deal with it. This betrays the gospel. It also betrays the possibility of our being changed by the message of Jesus.

The only proper response to the gospel and to its apparent impossibility is to accept it as it is and to focus on God. It is God who gives us the power to do what we cannot do by ourselves. The gospel repeats this theme often. It is God who makes it possible for us to live the gospel. We only experience this when we trust him and surrender to his power, allowing him to work in us. At the moment of surrender, we discover that what we thought was impossible has become possible for us through the power of God.

I keep forgetting the reality of my own powerlessness, Lord. I keep forgetting that my powerlessness doesn't matter, so long as I turn my life over to you. I offer you my poverty that I might receive your riches which allow your will to be accomplished in me.

NOVEMBER 4

Competition

Competition has a valid place in life, but in an egoistic society, it runs the risk of invading every facet of what we do. Competition can become destructive to our personal relationships. Our basic ways of relating become infected with exaggerated competitiveness, and we lose sight of the feelings and needs of others.

Our need to be competitive confronts us with interesting questions. For example, is it always necessary to have the last word in an argument? Can we sometimes admit that another person may have a valid point of view, even when it contradicts our own? Must we become personally deflated when we lose out in competition? Are our egos so fragile that we see ourselves as having worth only when we win? And finally, can we help others to achieve their goals without feeling personally diminished in the process?

It might be an interesting experience to live life simply for the joy of it, without making our years into a long series of competitive struggles. When people are no longer obstacles to be overcome, they can be appreciated simply for who they are.

Lord, give me the strength to moderate my competitiveness when it leads to egoism and a disregard for the feelings of others.

NOVEMBER 5

Who Are You?

If someone were to ask you who you are, you would probably give them your name. But that would not tell the questioner much about you at all. So you might be asked what you do to earn a living, whether or not you are married and have children, or perhaps, where you are from. Responses to those kinds of questions would reveal somewhat more about you, but many other questions would have to be answered before the picture of your identity could come into clearer focus. Knowing your personal tastes in literature and music would help someone to gain a further insight into the riddle of who you are. The sharing of your philosophical views and religious beliefs would reveal still more about you, and yet, the full story of yourself would not be found there either.

Jesus said, "you will know that I am in my Father and that you are in me, just as I am in you" (Jn 14:20). Through his life within us, we have become related to God. That is the most important reality we can assert about ourselves. It seems strange that, when we consider our identity, we rarely think of it in this deepest sense. Through God's goodness, we have become his children. Is there anything more profound that we can say about ourselves?

Lord, may I never forget who I really am.

NOVEMBER 6

Value Judgments

We sometimes value people according to how appealing they appear to us, how intelligent they are, how much money they make, what they contribute to society, how healthy they are, and finally — what they can do for us. People who fall outside of those categories become nonentities to us. But the gospel tells us that all human life is precious. All people deserve our respect because of their innate value.

When our love for others is based solely on our personal preferences, we no longer love according to the teachings of the gospel. If we cannot love those who fall outside of our personal preferences, how safe is our love for our friends? How will we continue to love them when they lose some of the qualities that first attracted us to them?

Not everyone can be a friend, but everyone must be affirmed as a person. Our love must touch everyone just as sunlight covers everything it shines upon. This is the way God loves, for his love touches everyone without distinction. Can you love this way? You will know when someone unattractive to you comes into your life and needs your help.

Lord, may I not shun the unattractive when I see them before me in need, for the measure of my love for them is the measure of my love for you. Help me to love as you do.

N O V E M B E R 7

The Unexpected

Things are not always what they seem to be, and events do not always turn out as we plan them. These statements may be truisms, but sometimes they catch us off guard. The twists and turns of life's surprises are going to touch us, no matter what we do. Some of the surprises may have a touch of comedy about them, while others will strike us as tragic. But there is an advantage to being open to the unexpected in our lives, no matter what form it takes. We survive more realistically when we are ready for it.

Our own misunderstandings create some of the twists and turns of life. Sometimes we miscalculate the meaning of others' actions. We mistake people's shyness for dislike, or awkwardness for stupidity. Eventually we discover that things are often different from what they seemed to be. The same can be true for events in our lives that we regard as personal setbacks or disasters. Time often proves that things are different from what we thought they were.

One has to be prepared for surprise twists because the unexpected seems to be such an integral part of life. If we miss the surprise twists, we miss the truth of life itself.

Lord, keep me from rigid perspectives and false judgments. May I remain open to the unexpected in my life, to all the twists and turns that make up its meaning.

NOVEMBER 8

Barriers

Jesus said to him, "If you want to be perfect, go and sell all you have and give the money to the poor, and you will have riches in heaven; then come and follow me." When the young man heard this, he went away sad, because he was very rich.

— Matthew 19:21–22

Every choice implies a gain and a loss. The loss is the price we pay for the gain. The man in the gospel story was unwilling to pay the price, unwilling to transcend the barrier of his riches so that he could follow Jesus.

The story loses its full meaning if we think it deals merely with material barriers. Sometimes attitudes can be harder to give up than possessions or money. Following Christ would also mean giving up our facades and illusions, our pretenses of being someone other than who we really are. It would mean giving up the illusion of independence. Following Christ would mean giving up any of our personal barriers that would prevent us from being his friends. We all have such barriers. Which of them are we most reluctant to give up?

Lord, you know my weaknesses. Help me to identify and give up the barriers that prevent me from following you.

NOVEMBER 9

Blessings

Jesus taught us to ask the Father's blessings for ourselves and for others. Such prayers bear fruit because they increase our own love and faith, and because they direct our spiritual energies toward others for their good. We ask for God's blessings, and yet, at every moment of our lives God's blessings continually touch us, just as sunlight touches the earth.

If God's presence and God's blessings are already within us, we might simply pray to become more aware of what is already present. Our prayer would take the form of thanksgiving and gratitude for the blessings that we have. While we need to ask for things because Jesus taught us to do that, we would come to realize that God's blessings are a constant given. God's blessings become fruitful within us to the extent that we become aware of their constant presence and as we grow in the understanding of our dependence upon them.

I frequently ask for your presence, Lord, but I already have it. My asking makes me aware of what you wish to continue giving. And so now I ask you to increase my awareness of what always is. You are continually with me, and for this gift I give you thanks.

NOVEMBER 10

Living Faith

"Why do you call me, 'Lord, Lord,' and yet don't do what I tell you?"

— Luke 6:46

People with living faith practice what they believe. With that criterion, you can evaluate to what extent your own faith is alive. A living faith bears the fruit of love in which thought and action become one.

People who profess faith in God's loving care, but distance themselves from the needs of others, profess a faith without life. If we do nothing at all to alleviate the poverty and suffering of others, how will our faith be life-giving? Such a faith is just a facade covering up our own emptiness and lack of love.

The power to maintain a life of living faith comes from God. A humble person knows this, and that is why only a humble person can experience the joy of a living faith. It is a gift from God which enables the willing recipient to put into practice what God asks of him.

Lord, help me to practice what you teach me through your word and through your Spirit which dwells within me. If I fail to do what you say, I will fail to know you, for I will cease to understand who you are.

Quarrels

An argument broke out among the disciples as to which one of them should be thought of as the greatest. Jesus said to them, "The kings of the pagans have power over their people, and the rulers claim the title 'Friends of the People.' But this is not the way it is with you; rather, the greatest one among you must be like the youngest, and the leader must be like the servant."

— Luke 22:24–26

The basis of most quarrels is a desire to dominate, to be right, to control. This is the opposite of what Jesus teaches. The person who follows Jesus is one who empties himself and serves. He lets go of himself for the sake of others.

Perhaps the letting go of the ego is the difference between a quarrel and the standing up for a principle. We have to stand up for principles simply because we have to stand up for what is just, for what is good and right. Quarrels begin when our egos become overly involved in our disputes.

Quarrels begin when we insist on being right in those areas of life where it does not really matter.

We need to learn the difference between standing up for what is right and arguing merely for the sake of protecting a fragile ego. When we forget the difference, we are likely to find ourselves wasting time in useless quarrels.

Lord, teach me how to respect myself and at the same time to look to what is good for others. May I have the insight to protect truth for truth's sake and not for the sake of my ego.

NOVEMBER 12

Nature

Our temporal future is bound up with the future of our fields, our trees, and our water resources, for on all of these, we depend for our existence. What happens to our environment eventually happens to us. There is a reason, then, for us to preserve and care for the milieu in which we live. We need to care for nature because nature nurtures us.

There is another reason to protect the world of nature that is so deeply a part of us. Nature is a gift of God. It speaks to us about its creator because it reflects his beauty. When we spoil nature, we spoil the reflection of God and disdain his gift.

It is up to us to conserve and protect resources, to use the things of this world wisely, to blend with nature rather than simply to exploit it. It is up to us to keep our environment clean, to respect it as God's gift, to make sure that God's image in nature is not sullied by the unthinking use of his creation.

Nature reveals your beauty, Lord. If I have had a part in marring that beauty, I ask forgiveness. Inspire me to use the gifts of nature wisely, and to understand my responsibility for protecting what you have given.

NOVEMBER 13

Peace in the Midst of Darkness

The true wisdom of life is in accepting those things that we cannot change. Our natural tendency is to rebel against the persons and events in our lives that displease us. Sometimes we grow beyond rebellion to a stoic acceptance, a grim resignation that shoulders life as a burden. Because such an acceptance looks at life as burdensome, it does not contain the peace that can bring a quiet sense of joy even in the midst of darkness.

One of the big challenges of life is to accept frustrations with a calm, peaceful heart. No one does this by himself or herself. This is a gift of God and we ask for it simply by admitting our powerlessness and by standing before God with open hands. A peaceful acceptance in the midst of life's frustrations lightens the heaviness that we sometimes experience during a troublesome day. Peaceful acceptance enables us to live more calmly, and frees us from becoming engulfed in a kind of negative thinking that blocks us from experiencing joy.

Lord, may I learn to live more peacefully in the midst of my frustrations. I want to remember

*that all things are passing, and that you walk
with me through the joys and sorrows of each
day.*

NOVEMBER 14

Confrontation

People often have a difficult time admitting that
something might be seriously amiss with those they
love. The difficulty seems more prevalent today
than it was years ago. But it would seem that potential problems bear the seeds of deeper tragedy
when troubled persons get permissiveness instead
of caring confrontation from those who love them.
People see the signs of serious problems in their
loved ones, but sometimes they ignore the meaning of the signs, quite often with disastrous results.
Reluctance to confront problems seems to be an attitude that characterizes all kinds of individuals who
should know better. Why do they take such permissive attitudes toward the ones they love?

People sometimes hope that time alone will
heal those who suffer from life's more serious problems. Do the stories of life tell us that healing usually occurs in this way? Or is healing more likely to
come through caring involvement from concerned
family members or friends? Perhaps we jeopardize
the happiness of those we love when a false kindness prompts us to avoid caring confrontations.

*Lord, give me the courage and the love to con-
front others when a caring confrontation seems
to be needed. Help me to be a healer rather than*

an enabler, for permissive enabling is often the enemy of love.

Presumption

How often are we presumptuous with time? We plan to reconcile ourselves to a friend, but — no hurry. We still have time. We want to develop a deeper life of prayer, but — no hurry. We still have time. We want to respond to the needs of the poor and lonely whom God has put into our lives, but — no hurry. We still have time. And then one day it is suddenly too late. We have no more time! The opportunity for carrying out our intentions is past, or death makes our good but culpably unfulfilled intentions irrelevant. Either way we lose. So do others who need us. Too often this is the way it is when we are presumptuous about time.

Sometimes we are presumptuous about life, believing that somehow, while we sit back and do nothing, everything will turn out all right. It is a belief that our efforts really do not count because everything works out in the end without us. This presumptuous attitude is the opposite of what Jesus taught when he commanded us to help one another. If we are presumptuous in this sense, we sell ourselves short, believing that our attempts to do good have no real value. We forget that every effort made with love has value, whether it succeeds or not. And we forget that goodness does not grow in the world when good people sit back and do nothing.

I ask pardon, Lord, because so often I failed to do the good that I could have done. I want to be more aware of those areas of my life where I can make a contribution for the good of others. May I not discount the value of my efforts, or presuppose that others will do what I fail to do.

NOVEMBER 16

Worry

"So do not start worrying: 'Where will my food come from? or my drink? or my clothes?' Your Father in heaven knows that you need all these things. Instead, be concerned above everything else with the Kingdom of God and with what he requires of you, and he will provide you with all these other things. So do not worry about tomorrow; it will have enough worries of its own. There is no need to add to the troubles each day brings."

— Matthew 6:31–34

If it were possible to convert all the energy expended in anxiety and worry into something productive, our world would be essentially transformed. But if that sounds like an exaggeration, we might at least examine the waste caused by our own anxieties and worries. How much energy have we siphoned out of our own energy reservoirs in order to feed habits of anxiety and worry?

Perhaps the worst cases of anxiety and worry stem not so much from concern about ourselves, but rather from concern about those we love. What a useless expenditure of energy! We have some control over our own lives, but what can we change through our worries about others?

If we know how to interpret our life experiences, they tell us of the uselessness of chronic anxieties and worries. Our freedom from worry begins when we become aware of a compassionate God who assures us of his care and love. Confidence in God enables us to love and trust in the midst of a life that will always present some amount of danger and risk, a life that will tempt us to worry.

Increase my confidence in you, Lord, and help me to see that worry wastes precious energy. May I grow in peacefulness and in trust.

NOVEMBER 17

Treasure

"Do not store up riches for yourselves here on earth, where moths and rust destroy, and robbers break in and steal. Instead, store up riches for yourselves in heaven, where moths and rust cannot destroy, and robbers cannot break in and steal. For your heart will always be where your riches are."

— Matthew 6:19–21

If our treasures are things that grow old and rust away, do our treasures eventually leave us poor and without meaning? Jesus invites us not to treasure things that ultimately make us poor, but to treasure realities that finally make us rich. The only treasure we can ultimately have without rust is the eternal treasure of nonpossessive love — the ability to love and enjoy God, persons, and things simply because of their loveableness. We have inklings of what that means whenever we experience the joys of genuine friendships. Lesser treasures can add enrichment to our lives if they are seen in perspective, but whenever we try to find ultimate fulfillment in them, they will always sell us short. Does your own experience tell you this?

Jesus invites us to see all things according to his perspective. Everything works to our good if we realize what our ultimate treasure is. When we find it, our hearts will let us know, for where our treasures are, there our hearts are too.

Lord, may my heart be in the right place. May I not try to seek ultimate fulfillment in those things that cannot give it.

NOVEMBER 18

Sacrifice

"For whoever wants to save his own life will lose it; but whoever loses his life for my sake will find it."

— Matthew 16:25

The word "sacrifice" may sometimes arouse thoughts of aversion and repugnance, but its basic meaning is "to make holy." In this sense, sacrifice means giving up those things that keep us from being holy or whole. It means letting go of anything that keeps us from belonging wholly to God. Sacrifice, or letting go, implies a kind of death so that we might grow into new life. In making a sacrifice, we let go of selfish life in order to be a part of divine life.

When parents sacrifice for a child, they forgo their own wishes in order to respond to the needs of the child. They die to themselves in order that their parental relationship with their child might spring into life. Something similar happens when we make sacrifices for anyone we love. And this is what happens whenever we make sacrifices for God.

Love always implies sacrifice, because love looks to the good of another. It is in letting go of ourselves that we discover our relationships with others, and through the letting go, we grow into a deeper experience of love and life. Perhaps this is why the gospel often speaks of sacrifice, because sacrifice is the language of love.

I'm sometimes afraid of sacrifice, Lord, because I look at it as a loss, instead of seeing it as a gain. May I understand that sacrifice leads to freedom from selfishness, and to freedom for love.

Dependency

"I am the vine, and you are the branches. Whoever remains in me, and I in him, will bear much fruit; for you can do nothing without me."

— John 15:5

Independence, self-determination, and self-reliance are all deeply ingrained in our culture, and most of us admire people who take charge of their lives. We sense an evident fact — without some initiative and personal responsibility, no one accomplishes very much. There is truth in that, of course, but does our life experience tell us anything about the need for a healthy reliance on others?

We should not expect others to do for us what we can do for ourselves, but we are dependent on one another in many different ways. We discover that fact anew whenever the car malfunctions, whenever we go to the supermarket for groceries, or whenever we experience a need for human love and understanding.

In our moments of crises, we understand more deeply the gospel message that we are dependent upon God. Even in our times of success, there are no strengths or talents that we have not received from God. Our very lives have been gratuitously given to us. The next time we ponder our successes, we might remember to be grateful to the God and to the fellow human beings who made them possible.

Lord, may I never forget what I owe to you and to those who helped me to be who I am. May I be thankful for all the support I still receive.

Forbearance

Often enough, life does not correspond to our image of what it should be. Spring flowers bloom late; people do not respond to us as we wish; life does not give us what we want when we want it. What a fertile field for frustration.

The wise person knows that only so much can be expected from anyone or anything at any given moment. If people are trying to do their best, we need to accept from them whatever they are able to give. With time, they may be able to respond more fully to our legitimate expectations. In the meantime, we look at them with compassionate understanding, for at the present moment, they can only be what they are.

The laws of time and growth apply just as well to ourselves. We become impatient with ourselves, but at the present moment, we too can only be what we are. God never asks more of us than we can give. That is the reality of God's compassion. Perhaps this is the kind of compassion we need to show to others and to ourselves. It is the appropriate response to the way we grow, to the way we are all touched by the process of time.

Lord, may my expectations of myself and of others be realistic. When others disappoint me, may I look at them more with compassion than with anger.

NOVEMBER 21

Wrappings

My brothers, as believers in our Lord Jesus Christ, the Lord of glory, you must never treat people in different ways according to their outward appearance. Suppose a rich man wearing a gold ring and fine clothes comes to your meeting, and a poor man in ragged clothes also comes. If you show more respect to the well-dressed man and say to him, "Have this best seat here," but say to the poor man, "Stand over there, or sit here on the floor by my feet," then you are guilty of creating distinctions among yourselves and of making judgments based on evil motives.

— James 2:1–4

The wisdom of long-standing human experience reminds us never to judge a package by its wrappings. Our evaluations of others are often based on such externals. When we evaluate others merely by their external appearances, we run the risk of discounting their worth, approaching them without dignity, and missing the real meaning of who they are.

People are gifts in our lives, and gifts come wrapped in all kinds of ways. Learning to discover treasures that lie behind plain externals is an art that people learn gradually, one that they perfect as they grow in maturity. It would seem to be an indispensable achievement. How many marriages have failed because people did not really know how to exercise this art? How many possibilities of friendship were lost because people allowed themselves to be sidetracked by the wrappings?

Lord, I want to love others as you see them. May I learn to look beyond the wrappings.

NOVEMBER 22

Sensitivity

Only if we care enough to understand other persons in their uniqueness can we adequately relate to them and respond to their needs. Without that understanding, we become insensitive and risk making serious mistakes in the way we relate to others.

The Bible portrays Jesus as a model of sensitive relationships, precisely because he was mindful of the uniqueness of others in his relationships with them. Jesus had only gentle words for the woman caught in adultery, because her humble admission of sin called forth his compassion and forgiveness. In contrast, Jesus' approach to the unrepentant and the self-righteous was stern. With them, a gentle approach might have been less effective than confrontation, and therefore less loving. Jesus' sensitive love gave him the ability to respond to people's needs as the uniqueness of their individual personalities and circumstances required.

If we are unaware of the uniqueness of others, we cannot relate to them as they are. Only those with sensitivity to the particular personalities of others know how to relate to them with love and to give them what they need.

Lord, may I care enough about others to be sensitive to their personalities and needs. Help me to imitate your way of relating to others.

NOVEMBER 23

Hidden Meanings

People's actions have a transparent quality about them when they are motivated by a sense of love. The love shines through their actions, but it is only discernible to those awake to its meaning. For example, a friend invites you to a meal prepared not only with culinary skill, but also with deep love and friendship. You can taste the results of the culinary skill, but are you aware enough to "taste" the love? The friend's meal contains a hidden meaning. Would such a meal have a quality different from a similar meal purchased at a restaurant?

In the same way, any gift given in friendship reveals more than just the quality of the gift itself. For one who knows how to look, the gift reveals the love of the friend who gives it. The tragedy is that such a way of seeing is so often overlooked. It depends on a certain vision of life that can only be developed with practice. Those who have the vision know how to discover the hidden meanings behind the seemingly ordinary events of life.

*Lord, I've frequently missed the hidden mean-
ings in the many acts of kindness people have
shown to me. May I become more aware of the
love contained in the acts of friendship which
I so often take for granted.*

NOVEMBER 24

Possessiveness

When you hold a little chick in the palm of your
hand, it is content to stay there. When you close
your hand around it because you are afraid it will
hop off, then it struggles to be free. That is the way
it is in our relationships with others. When we try
to possess them, they struggle to free themselves
from being smothered.

Personal relationships can only flower when
love is freely given and freely received. When we
love like that, we imitate God. In loving us, God
took a tremendous risk — he created us with free
will. We have a "smother-free" God who respects
our power to say no. He holds us in his hand, but
the hand is open, and our power to rest there freely
is the dignity we receive from God. Only a love
freely given and freely received can be meaningful
and life-giving.

Our own ways of loving may not be as life-
giving as God's ways. To the extent that we are
possessive, we squeeze life out of relationships that
should be vibrant and free. Sometimes we show our
possessiveness in our reluctance to let our loved
ones change. Change demands new ways of relating, letting go of what seemed sure, and accepting

anew that human friendships carry elements of risk.
Letting go does not mean the ending of a loving relationship. It simply means letting the relationship
rest freely on open hands. That is the best hope we
have for friendships to last and grow.

*Lord, may I let go of possessiveness and allow
others the freedom to accept or reject my friendship. May I be free enough to accept a no, for
without my willingness to take that risk, my
love will never be like yours.*

N O V E M B E R 25

The Need to Hear

It is possible to love others and never verbalize
what we feel. Yet, we all hunger for verbal assur-
ances. Even if we see the actions of love and caring,
we still want to hear the words. Are we sensitive
enough to say to others what they need to hear?

Jesus showed his love not only by living
among us, curing and healing, and dying for us, but
he also gave us the verbal assurance of his love: "I
love you just as the Father loves me; remain in my
love" (Jn 15:9). And Jesus received the verbal assurance of love from his Father: "You are my own
dear Son. I am pleased with you" (Mk 1:11).

Love's fullness demands expression, the expression of words in addition to the expression of
actions. People need to hear these words from us.
We might suppose that God enjoys hearing them
too. Do we care enough to say them?

*Lord, may I understand that love is meant to
be both seen and heard, and that my loved ones
need to hear the words from me.*

NOVEMBER 26

Doing Something for God

"I tell you, whenever you did this for one
of the least important of these brothers of
mine, you did it for me!"

— Matthew 25:40

God has no personal needs, so what can we give
him to show our love? The Bible tells us that God
has made himself one with those who do have
needs. Since God identifies himself with his people, in a mysterious sense their needs become his.

When we feed the hungry, spend time with the
lonely, and bring hope to the suffering, we minister
to the God who identifies himself with his people.
This is a great mystery, and it has been revealed by
God as an expression of his relationship to all of us.
It is a mystery not simply to be pondered, but to
be lived.

*Lord, may I more clearly understand that in
serving my brothers and sisters, I serve you.
Through the power of your presence in my life,
help me to respond to the needs of others.*

Disguises

"Woman, why are you crying?" they asked her. She answered, "They have taken my Lord away, and I do not know where they have put him!" Then she turned around and saw Jesus standing there; but she did not know that it was Jesus.

— John 20:13–14

Mary did not recognize Jesus. She thought he was the gardener. And when the apostles saw Jesus, they did not recognize him either. They thought he was some kind of ghost. All of these people had spent time with Jesus. Why were they not able to recognize him?

The appearance of Jesus was changed after the resurrection, because, through the resurrection, Jesus himself had changed. Those who had known him during his earthly life would have to discover him in his new way of being. Perhaps that is what the experience of Mary and the apostles teaches us. Jesus is very much with us after his resurrection, but he is with us in a disguised way. We have to penetrate the disguise. Mary had to see beneath the appearances of a gardener. The apostles had to see beneath the appearances of a ghost.

We have to see Jesus beneath the appearances of the poor and of those in whom we would least expect to find him. That is where he is. If we can find him there, we can find him in anyone. The risen Jesus is in each of us, and when we believe that, we can look inside and discover him even within ourselves.

Lord, you love disguises. May I not be fooled. You hide yourself deep within every human being. May I be wise enough to find you.

NOVEMBER 28

Gladdening the Holy Spirit

And do not make God's Holy Spirit sad; for the Spirit is God's mark of ownership on you, a guarantee that the Day will come when God will set you free. Get rid of all bitterness, passion, and anger. No more shouting or insults, no more hateful feelings of any sort. Instead, be kind and tenderhearted to one another, and forgive one another, as God has forgiven you through Christ.

— Ephesians 4:30–32

This is an exhortation to put away those things that poison our lives and destroy our ability to love. To sadden the Holy Spirit would mean to ignore our potential to do what God does. It would mean that we would choose selfishness instead of choosing love. It would mean being walled up in ourselves instead of being a part of the stream of love in which we experience God and discover communion with others.

If the Holy Spirit is saddened by our lack of love, the Holy Spirit must be gladdened by our choice to love in his image. To gladden the Holy Spirit would mean to live as he does, finding our identity by imitating God. By avoiding those actions and attitudes that destroy love, and by doing those actions that make love grow, we forge our identity in the image of the Holy Spirit who continually breathes his love into us.

Lord, may I always gladden your Spirit who lives within me. Show me where I block the flow of your love.

NOVEMBER 29

Love's Opposite

There is no fear in love; perfect love drives out all fear.

— 1 John 4:18

The opposite of love may not be hate, but fear. We all hunger for the experience of loving and of being loved, but something blocks us from reaching out to satisfy the hunger. The more we separate ourselves from healing love, the more we experience isolation and fear. The fear may show itself as an apprehension about future catastrophes, as worries and anxieties, as a discomfort with life that blooms into hostility toward others. Instead of loving others, we wind up feeling threatened by them. The spiral of fear grows and we become enmeshed in an inability to love.

Most of our fears stem from illusions about ourselves. We think we are not loveable, and so we

reality in you. May I never look at myself or at any of my brothers and sisters as ultimately hopeless, for that would deny the power of your love. Thank you, Jesus, for your loving acceptance which gives meaning and joy to my life.

DECEMBER 20

Words to Live By

Jews want miracles for proof, and Greeks look for wisdom. As for us, we proclaim the crucified Christ, a message that is offensive to the Jews and nonsense to the Gentiles; but for those whom God has called, both Jews and Gentiles, this message is Christ, who is the power of God and the wisdom of God. For what seems to be God's foolishness is wiser than human wisdom, and what seems to be God's weakness is stronger than human strength.

— 1 Corinthians 1:22–25

"Waste not, want not." "If you burn the candle at both ends, you are not as bright as you think." "Character does not reach its best until it is controlled, harnessed, and disciplined." Would these be words to live by? In all of them, there is a certain wisdom and truth, but they all fall short of the higher wisdom of the gospel.

The wisdom of the gospel is Christ crucified and Christ risen, a Christ we are called to imitate. It is a wisdom of self-forgetfulness. It may not seem to touch the issues of successful living as the world understands them. In fact, the words of Jesus may seem foolish to those preoccupied with possessions and power. Yet it is Jesus' words that invite us to genuine life by asking us to die to our selfishness. How else could we discover the way that leads to genuine love and union with others? Only those who live Jesus' words understand the full peace and joy that come to those who accept them.

May it always be your words, Jesus, that guide my life and give it its meaning. Through your light, may I come to see more clearly the wisdom they contain, and the peace they bring.

DECEMBER 21

Excuses

God purposely chose what the world considers nonsense in order to shame the wise, and he chose what the world considers weak in order to shame the powerful. He chose what the world looks down on and despises and thinks is nothing, in order to destroy what the world thinks is important. This means that no one can boast in God's presence.

— 1 Corinthians 1:27–29

If you are not wise according to the wisdom of the world, or influential, or exceptionally talented, should you excuse yourself from offering to others what you do have? It takes no great worldly wisdom to help a person in need, no influential position to listen to another's problems or share another's joys, no exceptional talent to spread a word of hope or encouragement. The wisdom and talents we have are sufficient for what God wants us to do. We are not excused from living life because our talents may not match the talents of those more gifted than ourselves. God wants us to use what we have. And that may be very important to those who need what we have to give.

You have given me, Lord, everything I need to love you, everything I need to do your will and to serve others. May I not look to the gifts of others, but appreciate my own, and trust in you that I will be able to use them as you wish.

DECEMBER 22

Being Positive

If you could eliminate all the negative aspects of your life, would you then become peaceful and relatively free from stressful feelings? Not necessarily. Without an awareness of the positive aspects of your life, you would miss the peaceful joy and contentment that keep you from unnecessary stress.

Being positive means being aware of your talents and gifts, being aware of the love and goodness you receive from others. Being positive means living with the hope that all of the promises of the gospel are completely yours. Being positive means being conscious of God's love and care which touch you at every moment of your day.

Without a deep awareness of the positive aspects of our lives, we lose sight of our own meaning. We become vulnerable to stress and we lose the peace that gives us our sense of well-being.

Lord, may I not take for granted the goodness with which you surround me. In the dark periods of my life, may my remembrance of your goodness bring me hope.

DECEMBER 23

Dignity

All through sacred history, God has chosen to need people in the realization of his plans for the world. He chose to need Moses in saving the Israelites from their slavery to the Egyptians. He chose to need the prophets in the interpretation of his word to his people. He chose to need Mary in presenting us with the gift of his Son. God chose people to work with him in accomplishing his will throughout the ages, and in this, he revealed the dignity of human beings.

More concretely, God has revealed your dignity by choosing you to help him accomplish his plans. He has willed to fill the hungry through you. He has willed to encourage the weak through you. He has willed to bring consolation and joy to others through you. God has chosen you as a trusted person through whom he wishes to work in the world for the good of others. What greater dignity can you have than to be chosen to work with your God?

Lord, I thank you for the dignity you bestow
on me by choosing me to work with you, and
to share in your caring for others. May I not
be unworthy of the trust you place in me.

DECEMBER 24

Christmas Eve

Here is a strange thing: God came to live among us, but there was no room for him to be born. It was not that he was rejected. It was just that nobody knew he had come.

God still wanders among myriads of human hearts, looking for a place to enter, for a place where he can share life and love. But often, he finds no room, for people are unaware that he is really present in the world. Christmas calls us to be aware of a gift, and the gift is God's offer to be with us, to love us, and to share our joys and sorrows. He is here. He is within you. This is the meaning of Christmas — God's giving of his presence, God's giving of his love.

Perhaps people are unaware of God's presence because he reveals himself in such ordinary ways. God chose to be born into an ordinary family. He lived among us in an ordinary way. Christmas is an invitation to find God in the ordinary, rather than in the spectacular. It is an invitation to find God in the daily love that people show to us, in the small acts of kindness and love that they offer to us without pretension. If we become conscious of the wealth of simple, ordinary love in our lives, we become conscious of the gift of God.

As I begin to celebrate your birth, Lord Jesus, may I become more aware of your presence within me and within the world. May I discover your incarnation in the ordinary events of my life.

DECEMBER 25

Christmas

"This very day in David's town your Savior was born — Christ the Lord!"

— Luke 2:11

God was well aware of our limits of spiritual understanding, and so he made his communication to us quite simple. He came among us as a baby, trusting and helplessly reliant on the goodness of human beings. That was God's initial communication to us in Jesus. That tells us something about God, the God who even now trusts us by allowing us to carry his life within ourselves. The message is simple, and we can understand it.

Of course, this is just the first of many messages. Many more are left to be uncovered. Jesus is a Christmas present from God, a present that is meant to be unwrapped so that it can be fully experienced and bring us joy. Christmas has no full meaning if the present is left wrapped. The question is whether we care enough about the gift to unwrap it, to savor it, to understand the giver in the gift. It takes years of prayer, love, and caring to fully unwrap the gift and to understand all of its messages. Christmas celebrates the beginning of the revelation of God's love in Jesus. We have a lifetime in which to deepen our understanding of the gift.

Thank you, Jesus, for the gift of yourself. I can never exhaust the mystery of your meaning, for your fullness will always elude my comprehension. May I spend my life deepening my understanding and my appreciation for who you are.

DECEMBER 26

Respect Life

Respect life! People usually use that term as a plea for respecting the life of the unborn. Could the term also be used as a plea for respecting the lives of those already in the light of day? The message of the gospel is about respect for the whole of life.

What if you found a person who respected the life of the unborn, but who did not care about the needs of those already born? What if you found a person who respected the life of the unborn, but who did not respect his family or community? What if you found a person who respected the life of the unborn, but who did nothing to ease the suffering and sorrow of those outside the womb? Following this line of thought, would we be the kind of people who fully respect life? Many of us find it easy to respect the life of the unborn. Our problem may be in respecting the lives of those who are already in the light of day. And here we have to start with our own families and communities.

When we allow selfishness or apathy to influence our relationships with others, we are not life-giving. Jesus tells us to love others as he has loved us. When we do this as completely as we can, then we fully respect life.

Lord, may I have the love and wisdom to respect the lives of others as I respect my own.

DECEMBER 27

Flying

When a bird matures, it tries out its wings, and it begins to taste the joy of flight. At first, the experience may seem unnatural, but once the bird knows flight, it will never simply remain bound to earth. It will often come back to earth, for that is a part of its life, but its satisfaction will never be complete unless it soars into the wind.

So it is with us. Once we taste the joy of knowing God through prayer and quiet, we will never be satisfied without it. We will often return to the busier aspects of our lives, our everyday activities, but we will never feel complete without the times of quiet communion with God. We discover that we need both of these experiences, activity and quiet, work and prayer, ordinary awareness and extraordinary awareness. We even discover that these two experiences enliven each other and that finally, they seem to become one.

There is no fullness without flying, no completeness without expanded awareness of God. And there is no expanded awareness of God without quiet prayer.

Lord, let me never forget that you have made me to fly.

DECEMBER 28

Yearnings

It is in the experience of our yearnings that we know we are fully alive. Without yearnings, we are like a bird that does not fly. Our yearnings define our lives. What are your deepest yearnings?

In our moments of honesty, we discover a sense of incompleteness in our lives. No matter how successful we are in the material world, it never fulfills us. We yearn for something beyond. Those who see this come to know the meaning of wisdom.

Our deepest yearnings are for the experience of belonging, the experience of communion that goes beyond what is visible and material. Our deepest longings are the longings of the spirit — the wish to be understood, to be accepted, to be one with God at the core of our being. And in our oneness with God, we long for oneness with each other. These are the yearnings that define us at the deepest level of our existence. We respond to them through prayer and through service to each other.

Lord, may my deepest yearnings be for you, and for communion with others in you.

Curiosity

Herod said, "I had John's head cut off; but who is this man I hear these things about?" And he kept trying to see Jesus.

— Luke 9:9

Herod was curious about Jesus. His curiosity aroused in him a desire to understand something of who Jesus was.

Without at least some curiosity, we will never have the interest to know more deeply who Jesus is. If the curiosity is motivated by love, then it will lead to a more personal understanding of who Jesus is for us.

A loving curiosity about Jesus is a gift, and it is a gift for which we ought to pray. To the extent that we have this gift and respond to it, we come to experience Jesus in our lives, and the personal meaning he has for us. The depth of our relationship to Jesus is born from a curiosity motivated by love. As we indulge more deeply in our curiosity, our love grows and begins to bear fruit.

Lord, I know that I will never fully understand you, but may my curiosity to know you more clearly never weaken or die.

Blessedness

"Happy are you poor; the Kingdom of God is yours! Happy are you who are hungry now; you will be filled!"

— Luke 6:20–21

Those people who seem to be blest in a special way are considered lucky. We usually think of blessings as things or circumstances that bring joy. That is true, of course, but sometimes the joy may not be what we think it is.

Jesus called the poor "blest." But what kind of joy would such a blessing bring? Why would those who hunger consider themselves blest? One needs to hear the promise of Jesus in order to get the answer. Blessings are those circumstances in life which lead us to God. A sense of our poverty leads to God if it results in an understanding that only God can fill us. How could anyone be filled by God if he is full of himself? Hunger leads to God if it results in an understanding that we are not sufficient for ourselves. And so in our neediness we are blest, not because our needs make us feel good, but because they open us up to the one who can fill us with what we truly need. Our needs can wake us up to what is most real in our lives. To that extent, they are blessings.

Lord, may I learn something from my needs. If they lead me to you, then they will truly be blessings in my life.

Endings

Tonight, this year comes to an end. Endings prompt different kinds of thoughts in each of us. We might look at this year and evaluate our successes and our failures. We might decide to give thanks for our successes, knowing that these were gifts of God, and we might decide to ponder our failures, knowing that there is something we can learn from them. Or perhaps we might simply want to give thanks for the gift of life that this year has brought to us.

Perhaps our mood shifts as we allow ourselves to focus on the gift of the new year. Today's ending is tomorrow's new beginning. Isn't this always the way of life? One thing ends that something else may begin. That is the law of growth. We see it take place in our own lives in so many different ways.

The ending of this year and the beginning of the new might remind us of the central message of the gospel. Our lives will never end, but they will be given a new beginning. What dies will rise up, and there will be a new way of being. And so we end this year with thankfulness for what was, and we anticipate the new year with hope for what will be, knowing that God's promises sustain us.

Lord, thank you for this year, for the love and the life which you have so graciously given to me. May my love and trust grow during the coming year so that I might learn more deeply about your wisdom, and experience more clearly the joy of your love.